THERE GOES MAINE!

BOOKS BY JOHN GOULD

New England Town Meeting
Pre-natal Care for Fathers
Farmer Takes a Wife
The House That Jacob Built
And One to Grow On
Neither Hay nor Grass
Monstrous Depravity
The Parables of Peter Partout
You Should Start Sooner
Last One In
Europe on Saturday Night
The Jonesport Raffle
Twelve Grindstones
The Shag Bag
Glass Eyes by the Bottle
This Trifling Distinction
Next Time Around
No Other Place
Stitch in Time
The Wines of Pentagoët
Old Hundredth
There Goes Maine!

WITH LILLIAN ROSS
Maine Lingo

WITH F. WENDEROTH SAUNDERS
The Fastest Hound Dog in the State of Maine

THERE GOES MAINE!

A Somewhat History, Sort of, of the Pine Tree State

JOHN GOULD

W · W · NORTON & COMPANY
NEW YORK   LONDON

The text of this book is composed in Janson, with
display type set in Goudy Bold. Composition and
manufacturing by the Maple-Vail Book Manufacturing Group.

First Edition

Library of Congress Cataloging-in-Publication Data
Gould, John, 1908–
There goes Maine! : a somewhat history, sort of, of the Pine Tree
State / John Gould :
p.   cm.
1. Maine—History—Anecdotes.   I. Title.
F19.6.G68   1990
974.1′00207—dc20   89–39139

ISBN 0-393-02834-8

W. W. Norton & Company, Inc.
500 Fifth Avenue
New York, N. Y. 10110

W. W. Norton & Company Ltd.
37 Great Russell Street
London WC1B 3Nu

1 2 3 4 5 6 7 8 9 0

*For Joe Novick, my longtime friend
and flyrod companion, and in memory
of his JoAnne, who died too soon,
and of the rum plum jam.*

PETER PARTOUT'S PAGE

Dear Mr. Editor:

A few years back I was visiting Chum Colby up to Anson, and while we were drinking supper Chum looks out the window and sees his carriage shed was afire. He cranked the telephone and the firemen came and did a good job. But just before Chum gave his alarm the firemen had loaded a big hog into the hose end of the fire engine. The hog belonged to Chief Perley Norton, and the boys were going to take it over to Ned Gaylord's— Ned did slaughtering. So along comes the fire engine, hog and all, and puts out Chum's fire. Then the reporter from the Madison *Bulletin* arrives, and when his story about the fire comes out in the paper he doesn't mention that hog at all. Not one word. You'd think that hog didn't have one thing to do with Chum's fire. If you see what I mean, I think this Gould fellow tells us a pig in a fire engine deserves notice, and might even be more important than the fire. Don't you feel that way? I do.

(Signed) *Peter Partout*

Peppermint Corner

"As goes Maine, so goes the Union."
—American political maxim, c. 1888

The original Maine constitution, 1820, called for state elections "on the second Monday of September biennially forever." Since the other states voted in November, the "early bird" Maine outcome could be prophetic. Usually it was, because in the days following the Civil War Maine had many sons in prominent positions in Washington, D.C., and Down-East philosophies did influence national policy. The maxim "As goes Maine, so goes the Union" was by no means an idle saying. But in 1957 the voters of Maine foolishly amended their constitution and began voting in November along with the crowd.

THERE GOES MAINE!

INTRODUCTION

"A history of Maine, you say?"

"Ayeh. Well—somewhat . . ."

"But why? What can happen in Maine? Away up there on the edge of nothing! Blueberries, fish, paper mills!"

The entire history of North America began in Maine. Nobody knows just when, but there was good reason why. Fish. The notion that piety and freedom to worship God nurtured our New World is poorly supported. Good State o' Maine cod, salted and in brine, was a staple in the markets of Europe well before any of the historically established explorers came looking for that elusive "passage" to Cathay. Any Irish fisherman could have told Columbus, Cabot, Hudson, even Jacques Cartier, that no such passage existed—that you couldn't reach the East Indies by sailing west up one of our rivers. A big continent in the way. He could have, that is, except that none of those schoolbook heroes had been born yet.

Off Sheepscot Bay the chart shows a group of islands named the Damariscoves. These islands were a rendezvous and fisheries station for Europeans long before any historian discovered America. In the year 1620, which brought the Pilgrims to Plymouth, thirty-two English vessels loaded fish there, and each vessel made several voyages during the summer season. The *Mayflower*, which would otherwise have been in that fleet, forewent the late fall trip because she was chartered to fetch the Pilgrims.

Now, better than halfway up from the tide on one of these islands is a stone wall—such as Maine farmers were to lay up later when they commenced clearing their fields. The rocks were piled to make fences. This wall on that island forms a circle and remains a mystery. A tremendous amount of work went into the building of it, and as it predates any attempt at farming out there—why? Why was it built out there? If it were built to keep animals in and out, what animals, and what would they be kept in and out of? For that matter, why fence animals on an island they couldn't leave anyway? If the wall were for defense, what did it protect and whom did it fend off? Could the thing have some ceremonial purpose, something like Stonehenge or the pyramids of Egypt? If so, what is the secret, and what priests came there to compute the angles? From where?

Nobody knows. The foolish wall was there when the first seafaring wanderers were blown in on a wind from Iceland, and when fishermen came later, they wondered. Columbus hadn't been born.

Historians make a poor lot for writing history. They like to stick to facts and accordingly miss a good deal. They never enjoy a wild surmise. Several esteemed books will tell you how many quintals of fish were flaked and brined and shipped from the Damariscoves, fetching so much at Liverpool. There are good descriptions of the facilities—wharves, derricks, drying stages, homes, and boat yards. There seems to be no good place that tells the curious about that wall.

There is a line in the biography of Christopher Columbus that every schoolchild has read. It says that as a lad he made a voyage as cabin boy to the British Isles. Thus far, no historian has ever set himself down to meditate on that and figure out what it means. That Columbus went to the British Isles is all right; the ancient Phoenicians sailed that route to get tin at Cornwall. But the ancient Phoenicians knew that when you came to the horizon your ship didn't drop off the edge of the earth. So what's this about smart Columbus propounding a brand new theory that the earth is round? If he'd pulled that in any congregation of mariners, somebody would have said, "So what else is new?" And when in the British Isles, Columbus certainly did what any sailor does in port, and without the slightest doubt he must have talked to somebody who had been to America. By that time almost anybody on a British waterfront knew about America, and most had been there. A good many had probably looked up at that stone wall and wondered. But back in Spain they hadn't gone for the fish, and Columbus had a bright idea that he presented to Queen Isabella. Give him credit.

By the time England got around to thinking about an empire, years had passed. They divided Virginia, named for Queen Bess in whimsy, into North Virginia and South Virginia, and set up two companies to colonize and develop. Each company was forbidden to exploit within 150 miles of the other. The part nobody wanted remained South Virginia, and North Virginia became New England. When the Pilgrims made ready to come to New England, they asked for permission to settle, but the older term "North Virginia" persisted in the records, and this led most historians to presume that they started for "Virginia" but perverse winds and poor seamanship brought them to New England by mistake.

This is utter balderdash. The *Mayflower* came on the precise course she would take for The Damariscoves, and made landfall right on the button at Monhegan Island. The skipper, an old hand at the fishing grounds, showed the Pilgrims how to put out their lines, and they caught "some coddes." The next day the *Mayflower* went on to Cape Cod, which was where the Pilgrims meant to go. Fact, which is not always reliable, says the Pilgrims had asked permission to settle in Maine, where the action was, but the proprietors felt their oddities might prove a distraction to the fish business, and the Pilgrims were told to go down to Massachusetts where they'd be out of the way. The only person who ever got lost that way in those days was Hendrik Hudson, who got too close to the magnetic pole, where his compass went sour. Perplexed him some.

About the time Columbus was making his pitch to Isabella, an Irish fishing boat drifted on a quiet tide into Monhegan. The season was late and the artists had gone, so the skipper wasn't sure if he was where he meant to be. But some Indians came rowing alongside in a lapstrake, round-bottom double-ender to set him straight, and he was pleased that they spoke very good English. They assured him that they were also fluent in French, and joshingly they cried out, "Ciad mille failte!" Everybody laughed. They said they had these boats custombuilt in Normandy, and they cost three beaver skins apiece. The skipper remarked on the clothing these Indians were wearing, and they gave him the name of their tailor in London. A suit with two pairs of pants cost one quintal of herring in brine, and the tailor shipped their orders regularly on the first boat each spring. There was a squaw over at Pemaquid who took care of alterations. Sometimes Indians from as far away as the Connecticut Lakes came to order clothes. These Indians told the Irishman that they'd heard the Spanish were planning to send out three boats to explore.

So it goes with historians. In Maine history, there is not only that mysterious wall on the island, but there is Alpheus Ruggles. Alpheus lived up West Minot way, and he was a great hand at building stone walls. Nobody could lay wall to match him. Somebody asked him one time how much stone wall he could lay in a day if he kept at it—lugging his own rocks. He didn't know, so one morning he purposed to find out, and he stepped right around all day, taking just a half hour for lunch. And lugging his own rocks. At twilight he quit, and it took him two days to walk home.

John Gould

Friendship at Muscongus, 1989

I

The discovery of North America by the Squareheads and how Leif Eriksson, also, was a come-lately. And how the *skrellings* did in poor Thorwald, Leif's brother, and made him talkative.

The first Europeans to visit Maine left us little to go on, for the reason that they didn't know where they were. It would be helpful if we could find in the small records some such phrases as "near Bangor," "not far from Wesserunsett," and "just downriver from Pejepscot." A great pity it is that we have no pinpoint way of knowing just where Thorwald lies buried in perpetual enjoyment of his spot. He had said, "This is where I want to stay," and he did.

Leif Eriksson, son of Eric the Red, was never the man who discovered America. It was quite some time before Leif that a "Northman" named Naddod got carried away by a vagrant gale and discovered Iceland. A Northman

was anybody out of Scandinavia—Swede, Dane, Nor-
wegian—and Naddod was not quite two hundred miles
out and had no idea where he was. This kind of unin-
tentional discovery was to go on for years. After the
wind died down, Naddod made his way back to Copen-
hagen, and a little time later some Danes followed up
on his remarks and found there was, just as he had said,
an Iceland. These Danes stayed there, waiting for another
gale, and when the wind picked up they went along
with it and found Greenland. About five hundred miles.
Iceland belongs to Europe and Greenland belongs to
North America. North America had been discovered.

This makes the methodical approach to discovery, as
pursued by Christopher Columbus, seem a trifle tedious. All anybody has to do is wait for a strong wind.
The Danes who thus got blown to North America
returned to Iceland after the storm, but not until they
had looked around some and had found Labrador,
Newfoundland, Nova Scotia, Maine and Swampscott,
Massachusetts. Then came Leif Eriksson, who touched
at Maine somewhere between Eastport and Kittery, and
moved around Cape Cod to spend a winter in Rhode
Island. Later, but not much later, Leif's brother Thorwald followed Leif's directions and he, too, stayed over
at Newport, using the accommodations Eric had left. It
was on his way back to Greenland and Iceland, and
Denmark, that Thorwald changed his plans and decided
to stay in Maine.

He had anchored his vessel, the *Thorberg Skafting*, in
a quiet harbor and was making wassail amidships with
his crew when the masthead lookout sang down, "Ay
tank ay ban see boa-oats!" It was so—between the *Thorberg Skafting* and the shore, three canoes were passing,
each bearing three Indians. That's nine. Just for the fun

of it and because there was nothing else to do at the time, Thorwald had a boat lowered and his men rowed him in pursuit of the canoes. Before the Indians knew just what was happening, eight of them were dead. Good sport. The ninth escaped ashore and was later run down and caught by some of his friends in the neighborhood of Albany, New York.

On the way back to the ship after this amusing interlude, Thorwald looked about at the entrancing beauty of the snug harbor, the dark and pointed spruces against the cerulean sky, and he said, "It's so lovely here I'd like to spend the rest of my days right in this magnificent spot!"

It was perhaps half past six, going on seven, the next morning that the masthead lookout sang again, this time with, "By Odin and by Thor—lookit all the geedee Indians!" His alarm came none too soon, for the *Thorberg Skafting* was surrounded by canoes, each full of Indians, and in about two minutes they'd shot so many arrows the *Thorberg Skafting* looked like a porcupine (hedgehog). Thorwald and all his men (the lookout had shinnied down the mast in time) hid below decks and behind beer kegs on the deck, and upon seeing that their arrows were having no effect against the stout planks and staves, the Indians withdrew, their arrows exhausted. There was but one casualty aboard the *Thorberg Skafting*. An arrow had by simple chance found a mark—Thorwald himself had been pierced below his armpit and above his flagon. He lived just long enough to utter the most improbable last words in the long history of last words. So help us Johanna! It is on record in *History of Maine* by Abbott that he said, blood gushing from his wound and the arrow point painfully imbedded in his vitals,

This is my death-blow. I strongly advise you to depart as soon as possible; but first take my body to the shore and bury it upon the promontory before you. There I had intended to make my abode: I shall now dwell there forever. Place two crosses at my grave,—one at the head and one at the foot; and let the spot, in all future time, be called The Promontory Of The Crosses!

So saying, he expired, and it was done. The word "cross" appears in Maine place-names twenty-two times, and no doubt the spot where Thorwald lies forever is included in that number. His grave commemorates the first fight between native Mainers and people from away.

Five or six years later, one of Eric's sons by the name of Thorstein came to Maine and brought his wife Gudrida. He died later in Greenland and once back in Scandinavia Gudrida married one Thorfinn. He was well-to-do, and as she expressed a desire to visit Maine again he brought her back. He outfitted three ships for the trip, and they carried a hundred and fifty men, in addition to himself and Gudrida. Next came still another Thor, called January Thor, who discovered in reverse. That is, while he was in the Gulf of Maine a wind hit his boat and blew him all the way to Ireland. The Irish subdued him and his men and made slaves of them. Thus Ireland was discovered in 1010.

When the Scandinavians first saw Eskimos in Greenland, they called them *skrellings*, which means "little people." When they found Indians down in Maine, they used the same word for them. This offended the Indians, and in retaliation they called the Northmen "squareheads," a jocular sobriquet that persists to this very day.

2

A short dissertation relating some
of the experiences endured by
Olive Hutchins of Chelmsford,
Massachusetts, in the year 1782
as she came to Maine to be a
pioneer mother, and how her
baby was taken by an Indian.

What kind of people settled the State of Maine?

If you remember, the British surrendered at York-
town in 1781. Captain Samuel Hutchins, then of
Chelmsford, Massachusetts, had commanded a company at the Battle of Bunker Hill, and so would be entitled to his soldier's bonus of a lot of land up in the
"district" of Maine. In 1782 his wife, Olive (she was a
Robbins), decided to strike out and take up this lot of
land, so's to have it ready for a home when Samuel got
his discharge. Olive was thus working her way up the
Kennebec River in May of 1782, proceeding slowly.

Very slowly, indeed. It was quite a trip. At the time there were four Hutchins children; the youngest was a baby. Mrs. Hutchins had persuaded (*hired* may be a handier word) an Indian to guide her up into Carrabasset Valley, and he was paddling a bark canoe with the four children, the wangan, and what household effects could be added to the load. Olive was walking along the bank of the river abreast of the canoe, leading a cow. This certainly makes the voyage of the Pilgrims sound like a Sunday School picnic, and to Olive the crowded comforts of the *Mayflower* would have been POSH indeed. Olive was not a big woman, but she was wiry and loaded with vigor and vitality, and she kept the cow stepping right along. She would hold her own among the mothers of Maine.

Things were going rather well on that trip up the river. Every so often Olive would pause to milk the cow and feed the baby. The other three children were able to do some things for themselves, and the Indian was proving a good guide and an amiable companion. He would make a comfortable camp each evening and keep a smudge for the blackflies, and he took game so the party had fresh meat. Olive's expedition reached Shoogun Falls and all was well.

But the next morning the Indian was gone. He had not only deserted, but he had taken the baby with him. Vanished.

Otherwise, it was a beautiful morning. The birds sang and the trout leaped, and a deer came down to teach her fawn to drink. There was no sense in sorrow or despair, so Olive milked the cow, tried not to think about feeding the baby, and fixed good breakfasts for the other three youngsters. Then she pressed on. She led the cow a distance upstream, tied her to a tree, and then came back down to bring up the canoe. She didn't try to paddle or pole, being slight of build, so she "frogged" the canoe along, pulling it by the bow and being careful not to mishandle the children or the cargo. Then she would tie the canoe and go back to bring up the cow. She did this for three days, and was pleased that she had to portage only twice.

On the fourth day the Indian returned, bringing the baby. The baby was perfectly all right—happy and gurgling, showing no abuse whatever. The baby was chewing on a chunk of porcupine fat with a string tied to it. This was a pacifier, and the other end of the string was tied to one of the baby's big toes. When the baby swallowed the pacifier the natural reaction was to choke and kick, and up would come the chunk of porcupine fat to start all over again. The Indian did his best to explain that he'd taken the baby over the mountain to show it to the squaws. They'd never seen a white baby.

Not many days after that, Olive decided to camp permanently on a pleasant intervale, and after the Indian helped her get settled he left. Before cold weather Captain Hutchins came home, and great was the family reunion. But before the captain returned, there was another incident that involved the cow. One night the cow blatted unduly, and Olive and her older son, Asamuel, rushed to the cow shelter to find that a wolf had somehow managed to get inside. When the wolf turned from the cow to make a lunge at Asamuel, Olive swung her ax and did the wolf in.

Perhaps fatigued by his war duty, Captain Hutchins lived only into his 42nd year, dying on a Christmas. Olive worked the farm and continued her widowhood for some years, but was later smitten by a short-frocked minister of some splinter group, and in her late sixties she married the parson. Again she was widowed, and lived another ten years, into 1836. Her tombstone says:

> Here lies a mother who was good,
> Who ever did whate'er she could . . .

Requiem for a true Maine mother.

3

It seems the people of Maine weren't any better then than they are now, but nobody is going to argue that they were uninteresting; Captain Jocelyn figured there were about six thousand of them, of which five hundred took their drams at Pemaquid.

So tell us some more about the kind of people who settled the State of Maine.

Anybody with a boat is a captain, and Captain John Jocelyn had a boat. He sailed along "The Maine" in 1670 and left us a report on what he saw. Kittery, he said, was then Maine's largest settlement, and next York and Wells. That makes sense in 1670, because they'd be closest to Boston, but today we think of those places as being just barely one of us. Jocelyn spoke of Winter

Harbor, which would be in the Saco area, and presumably thought it was a seasonal port. It was, instead, named for an earlier settler, one Mr. Winter. Jocelyn found Spurwink, Scarborough, Richmond Island, and Portland doing rather well. He tells how each settlement has "scattering" buildings, various gardens, defenses, and as he worked along to the eastward he mentions more and more fish stages and flakes. Saco, he said, had a sawmill. Portland had corn mills, and some eight hundred sheep. But eastward of Casco Bay he didn't find too much. The region from the Sagadahoc River to Nova Scotia was dismissed as "The Duke of York's Province," and he doesn't mention any French. He did mention Monhegan, Matinicus, Pemaquid, and Newagen—he spelled Newagen the old way, Capeanawhagen. At these places, he wrote, fishermen annually take hundreds of quintals of groundfish. They had, of course, been doing that for a good long time.

The total population from Kittery to Penobscot Bay was not more than six thousand in Jocelyn's day. But in the century before Jocelyn, there had been a shift from east to west—in 1628 Pemaquid had some five hundred residents and was the important American port. Pemaquid was even bigger and busier than Quebec City. But as Boston prospered, the closer settlements—Kittery, York, Wells—grew and Pemaquid declined. Now, many, many years later the English historian Arnold Toynbee was to dismiss Maine as an unimportant place inhabited by farmers and fishermen, and everybody got mad at him and wouldn't put his book in the liberry. Interesting that in 1670 Captain Jocelyn had written: "The people of the Province of Maine may be divided into magistrates, husbandmen or planters, and fishermen. Of the magistrates some be loyalists and others perverse."

Nobody in Maine has ever been reluctant to speak disrespectfully of judges, and a "perverse" magistrate would be one who didn't take his hat off if you mentioned the king. As to the farmers and fishermen, Jocelyn went far beyond any slurs by Toynbee: "They be alike. They have a custom of taking tobacco, sleeping at noon, sitting long at meals, sometimes four times a day, and now and then taking a dram." There is no record that anybody—judges, farmers, fishermen—read Jocelyn and got mad.

The perversity that Jocelyn described was a posture of indifference rather than animosity. That is, to be disinclined toward the Crown didn't mean you were palsy-walsy with the Bostons. The thoughts of rebellion and Americanism were to come later, and even then plenty of Mainers remained Loyalist. There was a Reverend Robert Jordan, Episcopal clergyman at Spurwink, who preached one Sunday and said, "The governor at Boston is a rogue and all the rest thereof rebels and traitors against the King!" He was promptly yanked before a grand jury, but then somebody began to wonder if perhaps he mightn't prove his words, and they dropped the case. The governors at Boston have always been leery of the truth, particularly as practiced in Maine.

People from Europe had been on "The Maine" for maybe five hundred years before the place was "discovered," but they came and went with the fishing and trapping seasons. The first to stay over were French, who had dreams of empire before England woke up. When the English woke up and sent people to catch, cut, and cure fish, they called them "planters," to allay (possibly) any French suspicion that competition was afoot. The settlers who tried to tame the Popham sand spits were planters, and Popham was a plantation. The word "plantation," for a semi-organized municipal division, is still used in Maine. Monhegan is a plantation, not a town. The humor of calling Popham a plantation is appealing—there would have been little demand in 1607 for wild cucumbers, juniper bushes, hardhack, eelgrass, and the other vegetation for which Popham soil is ideal.

When Captain Jocelyn described Maine people in 1670, he said more or less of what had been said back in 1630:

> These men were generally reckless adventurers. Some were runaway seamen, some fugitives from justice, and some those vagrants from civilization who, by a strange instinct, seek seclusion from all civil and religious restraints. The state of society was distinguished by its lawlessness. Every man followed his own impulses unchecked. The greatest immoralities prevailed. The Indians were cheated and outraged in every way which avarice, appetite or passion could incite depraved hearts. There was no sabbath here; no clergy to proclaim the gospel of Jesus Christ, with its alluring promises and its fearful retributions.

Things were so bad that the parent Plymouth Company took steps—not so much to bring its "planters" from their wicked ways, but because immorality was a sapping fault in the work force and bad for business in the long run. A three-man commission was sent from England to The Maine to bring some law and order, and possible piety, to the depraved people. The do-gooders were Robert Gorges as governor, Francis West as admiral and enforcement officer, and the Reverend William Merrill, Episcopalian, who would bring the miscreants to their knees and teach them better ways. This commission was given absolute power in all matters—capital, criminal, civil, military, and religious. But this effort wrought no reform along the Maine coast, and the first one to give up was the Rev. Merrill. His efforts to win respect for God and church won him jeers and hoots, and he abandoned the whole enterprise and went back to England in disgust. He reported that the situation was hopeless.

But the iniquitous Mainers seemed able to live with their own vices in harmony. The five-hundred-odd folks at Pemaquid would likely have brought their port along until it was the number one city on America's east coast—but during the French and Indian troubles good Mother Massachusetts neglected to defend her outposts, and Pemaquid was destroyed. Pity. In 1630 Pemaquid was no place to walk the streets after dark, but the folks there occasionally took a dram, and lingered pleasantly at table for four square meals a day.

4

The story of submission, and how Taxachusetts put the first bite on Mainers with sixteen shillings every time they opened a keg at the William Everett tavern in Eliot, thus *possibly* deterring the citizens of Eliot from tippling.

Kittery is Maine's oldest town, being first across the Piscataqua River from that part of America known as "away." At first the towns of Kittery and Eliot were the same. And it was in that part of Kittery now called Eliot that people met on the sixteenth of November, 1652, and "submitted" to Massachusetts. Just why anybody in Maine at that time, enjoying the finest kind, would want to pledge allegiance to Puritan Boston brings to mind Orrin Blethen of Dover-Foxcroft, who was 102 years old when he got married. Orrin didn't want to get married; he *had* to. And in 1652 it did seem wise, what with this and that, to join Massachusetts, although nobody at Eliot who signed the agreement really wanted to. (By the way: One of our Maine public television stations asked on a quiz show how many Maine counties derive their names from the Indians. All the contestants included Piscataquis in their answers, and the quiz master said, "Correct!" "Piscataquis" and "Piscataqua" are not Indian names. Look up *piscatus* and *aqua* in a Latin dictionary.)

During the first half of the seventeenth century there were some odd antics in Europe. France, Spain, and England kept having squabbles over territory, religion, matrimony, and trade, and in England the complications included popery and episcopacy, with the Puritans and the Presbyterians helping out whenever possible. After James and Charles came the Interregnum and Oliver Cromwell, the Great Protector, who rode in on six horses all at once and took over. So much was going on that it was not a good time to be a colonist over in America, and time and again when Mother England might have shown some interest the letters from the colonists went unanswered. The folks along The Maine had been on their own since Sir Ferdinando Gorges (he was an Episcopalian) eased off, and because they were Puritans the Bostons had little clout in the Rome versus Canterbury caper. But when Oliver Cromwell took over, the Puritan situation in New England seemed rosy indeed. All at once Boston thought it would be smart to take over Maine, so the General Court on Beacon Hill decreed that "the town of Kittery and many miles to the north thereof is comprehended within the Massachusetts Grant."

It so happened that nobody in Kittery or in the many miles north of thereof comprehended anything of the sort, and for a good reason—they held title to their lands under the old Gorges Grants, some had them from Henri of France Grants, some had them from Indians, and a good many just had them and the hell with Boston. But Massachusetts looked right then like a comer, and it seemed likely her Puritanism would pay off. Regardless of what the Mainers felt toward the Puritans—most Mainers were Episcopalian—prudence suggested a second thought. Now comes the decree from Boston that Mainers will be required to "submit" to Massachusetts in order to have their land titles "confirmed." Mainers would naturally receive equal benefits, and so forth.

Puritanism was no laughing matter. The Bostons had come to America all red hot over freedom of religion, but once settled in they permitted no religion but their own. They were pretty nasty about that. So while they could annex Maine at a profit, and could offer Mainers numerous benefits—military protection for one—the first thing to be done was convert all the Mainers to Puritanism. The land titles were the big argument—if Massachusetts were to dominate, a good and sufficient deed recorded at Boston would make sense. Mainers could see the reasoning behind this, and they weren't all that concerned over religion anyway. Why not? So the inhabitants of Kittery (and Eliot) were the first to be approached, and a commission was sent up from Boston to take their depositions, sign them up as "submitting," confirm their deeds, and accord them all the equal rights. Said inhabitants did assemble on said date of November 16, 1652, at the tavern of William Everett, which had a good kitchen and an excellent cellar and was a dandy place to meet. And said commissioners did arrive and said business was attended to.

One of the commissioners was named Bryan Pendle-

ton, and he was to dominate all the submission meetings that followed, farther to the east along the Maine
shore. He was to become the ancestor of all the ubiq-
uitous Pendletons of seafaring fame out of Searsport. At
one time something like fifteen Pendletons had their
vessels come into Liverpool Harbor on the same tide.
But in Searsport, during the busy days of tall ships,
long after submission to Massachusetts was purely historical, all the Pendletons denied this relationship and
said, "We don't speak of him." That's what Mainers
thought of Massachusetts and submission. Bryan Pendleton was no doubt competent at the job he had to do,
but he was arrogant, full of his own importance, and
needlessly discourteous to Mainers.

The meeting at William Everett Tavern was unruly.
The necessity of embracing Puritanism as a requisite to
a deed seemed irrelevant, as it surely was, and everybody said so. One man, John Burley of Kittery, told
the commissioners off in bold and fiery words, and
thought up a whole new batch of crimson adjectives for
Massachusetts and her commissioners. He had to be
restrained and removed from the hall, and the commissioners were going to have him tried for sedition and
related indiscretions, but they let him go when he agreed
to sign. Forty men and one woman did sign, no doubt
with adequate mental reservations, and thus submitted.
The woman was Mary Bachellor, and it has been said
that she gave Nathaniel Hawthorne his idea for Hester
Prynne in *The Scarlet Letter*. It might be; Mary Bachellor
was a minister's wife and later divorced him.

Pendleton held many meetings up the coast after that,
but the farther he got from Boston, the less pressure he
was able to exert and the harsher grew his receptions.
There's one story that he scheduled a meeting and

ordered everybody in town to come, and at the appointed time one lone fisherman appeared. The fisherman didn't show much respect—when Pendleton called the meeting to order the fisherman stood with his back to Pendleton and looked out the window to indicate his disinterest. Pendleton ordered the man to turn around and asked him why he was so disrespectful. The fisherman said he wasn't disrespectful, he was just looking up the road to see if anybody else was fool enough to come.

One result of submission and the equal application of the rights and privileges was immediately evident. After the tavern meeting landlord William Everett had to pay sixteen shillings' tax to Massachusetts every time he broached a butt. In 1910, when the town of Eliot observed its centennial, there was some irony in the program. A play was presented to reenact that submission meeting at the William Everett Tavern, and the curtain rose to reveal landlord Everett and his wife, with a number of Eliot citizens, seated at a table before the tavern "eating and drinking." While they were eating and drinking the commissioners arrived from Boston. It was a good play. Then, in the big centennial parade, one of the "floats" was a beautiful bit of work, all in white, provided by the Women's Christian Temperance Union. The W.C.T.U. was ever vigilant to remove all taxes on spirits by the simple elimination of spirits. The W.C.T.U. float won first prize.

5

A documentary of the short but useless life of a poor boy from "The Valley" who sought his fortune in far places, but came home again after making a great deal of money that never did him the slightest good.

For seventy beautiful miles the St. John River is the boundary between the United States and Canada. On both sides live descendants of the displaced Acadians from Nova Scotia who did not make the long trip to Louisiana with Evangeline Bellefontaine. At the time of the "great dispersal" in 1755 the first settlers of "The Valley" moved up the St. John River and started new lives—remaining quite apart from other activities in the United States and Canada. In the early 1800s the first English-speaking settlers came from "outside" to take up farms among the Acadians, and even today the proud descendants of the original French will explain that they are not "French-Canadians"—that is, they are not *habitant*. They do not use the word "Cajun," as in the bayou country, but distinctly say "Acadien," which is the eastern Indian name for the homeland of New Brunswick, Nova Scotia, and Maine. "Cajun," of course, derived from "Acadien."

The French of the Acadians in The Valley has been dissociated from Mother France since the days of Montesquieu, which means that modern French includes words these descendants do not know. More than likely, anybody in The Valley will tell you he "climbs the ladder" instead of saying he "goes upstairs." Every log home in The Valley had an *échelle* to reach the sleeping loft; it would be many years before the *escalier* was introduced. The Valley is still the remotest part of Maine. It is even remote to Aroostook County, and that's remote! And The Valley is still French—it will be helpful to bring a smattering if you visit St. Francis, Allagash, Lille, Frenchville, Fort Kent, Madawaska and other villages there. As well as places like Edmundston and St. Leonard on the Canadian side.

The story from The Valley that has been selected to round out and embellish this history of Maine is an improbable one, and concerns John Stadig, who was born in St. Francis. It is now necessary to explain that there are two towns in The Valley, directly across the river from each other, the one in Maine being St. Francis and the one in Quebec being St. (san) François. The towns are at the confluence of the St. Francis River, which flows out of St. Francis Lake in Quebec. The name "Francis" comes from the great Monsignor Montmorency, a churchman active in the early days of Quebec—his first name was François. When you go downriver from Quebec City on the North Shore to see the basilica at Ste. Anne de Beaupré, you will pass Montmorency Falls, a sheer drop of over 250 feet, which makes hydropower for Quebec City. Few people who gaze at the beauty of the cascade pause to think of the towns of St. Francis and St. François. Or of John Stadig, who was a native of St. Francis, Maine.

In the late 1920s John Stadig was working in the freight yards of the Bangor & Aroostook Railroad at St. Francis, but was living in St. François. This is important to the story because of customs regulations. The situation in The Valley has always been loosely construed by the officials of both countries, and what might be termed smuggling elsewhere is no more than a fact of life there. When the St. John River is frozen in the winter, international trade is very easy to come by. So with a home in St. François and a job in St. Francis young John Stadig faced the life of quiet desperation common to the area, and nobody supposed he would amount to much.

But one day in Fort Kent a cashier in a bank was talking to an agent of the Treasury Department, and he idly said he was curious about a fellow who kept coming in to exchange money. He wanted new twenty-dollar bills and wouldn't take any that had been folded. The cashier had asked him why, and he said he had a new wallet and didn't want to put dirty money in it. The Treasury agent said, "You don't say!" and began a few inquiries in a discreet manner.

Thus John Stadig began to be watched, and the United States Secret Service started a folder. They found that he had ordered certain things by mail, delivered at Fort Kent, and had taken his purchases into Canada without a declaration. The items he bought had to do with photography and possibly printing. But the laws of the

United States of America are not necessarily in force a hundred yards away in Canada. The Secret Service had to be careful, and needed a Canadian policeman. When a Quebec constable went to John Stadig's home in St. François, a U.S. Treasury agent went along as an observer only. They found Stadig had some good photographic equipment and supplies and a small printing press. And some printing plates for twenties and ones. The constable and the agent agreed they had found a counterfeiter.

But John Stadig said he was studying to be a lithographer and he hoped people wouldn't jump to an unjustified conclusion. When he realized this explanation was not being accepted, he offered the Treasury agent a thousand dollars if he would go away and forget everything. There has got to be something ludicrous in the very idea of accepting a cash bribe from a counterfeiter, and we should not be astonished that the agent declined. True, Stadig was red-handed in possession, he had taken undeclared goods into Canada, and he had tried to bribe an officer, but he had not passed any bogus money, and he was in St. François and not in St. Francis. Canadian justice was not in sync with United States law, so Stadig got only a few days in the local pokey and he was soon out. But all across the United States his name, description, and record were on file; John Stadig was a marked man.

He showed up next in Los Angeles, California. The Secret Service tailed him, waiting for him to perform. Next he moved to Las Vegas, where they jumped him, but a trifle too soon. They found glass negatives of money and some copper plates, but Stadig had not put any funny money in circulation. He was given only eighteen months, with credit for the time he'd been jailed to await trial. When he got out of the Nevada pen he came back to The Valley.

Stadig behaved himself for a few months, but in 1933 reappeared in Los Angeles. He picked up with the same people and began again where he left off. So did the Secret Service agents. He then popped up in Chicago and this time passed a ten-dollar bill, so they got him for real. But a week later he was being taken from jail to the federal courthouse when he jumped the paddy wagon at a traffic tie-up and took off up an alley. The frustrated agents found no trace until a few weeks later: phony twenties appeared in Portland, Oregon, and the laboratory said it was able to smell Stadig. However, this time Stadig hadn't passed the money—the two men arrested for doing so said they never heard of Stadig.

Next a printer in San Francisco reported to police that a man had come to him to ask about printing from copper plates, and he said yes, that's a picture of the man. Stadig. So Stadig was in San Francisco, and now the Secret Service boys came in force and picked him up on New Year's Day, 1934. The usual photographic and printing equipment was found, but this time Stadig had a roll of counterfeit twenties in his pocket. He got six years at McNeil Island. But five years and eleven months before he was to be discharged, he clobbered a guard and broke out.

Stadig was picked up the next day and was to be transferred to Alcatraz for higher security. But the curious workings of the United States judiciary system gave Stadig another chance. The indictments against him in Portland still stood, so he was taken to Portland to face them. There, another fifteen years were tacked onto his sentence, but on the way to Alcatraz on the train he jumped his guard and also out a window. By the time the train stopped, Stadig was beyond finding. But he had been badly scraped when he hit the ground, and he gave himself up after a few days. At Alcatraz finally and with years to serve, he went into a mental decline, and in September of 1936 the doctors decided he should be put in a hospital for defectives—this one in Springfield, Missouri.

Off he went with an ample guard, and on the way he spent a night at Leavenworth Penitentiary. On the morning of September 25, 1936, he was found dead in his cell. He had broken his eyeglasses and had used a fragment to slit his jugular. His body was sent to St. Francis and buried there. He had wandered, but he had come home. He was twenty-nine years old.

Like many another great man, Stadig had worked hard and had made a lot of money. He died penniless.

6

A brief narration of a colonial
incident that shows God was not
always on the side of the Indians,
even in the valley of the
Meduncook River, which is 6.5
miles long and flows into the
Atlantic Ocean.

A perennial hazard on the Maine farm was getting the
hay wet. Today, with machinery, hay is processed dif-
ferently, and the tedious way of mowing it with a scythe,
raking by hand, turning and tedding with a fork, and
then bringing it to the barn by horse and rack is happily
out of style. The very worst thing that happened in the
old days was to have the hay just right for carting from
the field and an afternoon thunder shower rip the heav-
ens open and souse the fragrant hay until it was soggy.
That meant waiting for the next dry day, spreading the
wet hay in the sunshine, tossing it up and over until it

was thoroughly dry—doing again what had been done before. And always with the possibility of another shower.

Back in the days of the French and Indian Wars, Maine settlers ran a constant risk of Indian attacks. In some places blockhouses gave shelter, and scattered homes had shutters and bars, and everybody kept a musket handy if need arose. On the shore of the Meduncook River, in what is now the town of Friendship, a remote family was making hay in the field one lovely July day when some Indians appeared, and the Indians didn't look too friendly. The family withdrew to the house, pulled the shutters together, barred the doors, and waited. The Indians turned out to be unfriendly, and shot a few arrows at the house and wasted a couple of musket balls on the heavy plank door. The family huddled in a corner and prayed.

Finding they could not get into the house easily, the Indians retired, and went into the hay field and brought hay to pile it around the house. It was nice, dry hay, and was fragrantly sweet from the July sun. When the Indians got hay piled all around the house, they set fire to the hay and went back a distance to sit down and watch. Smoke soon rose into the sky.

Just at that time the July thundershower struck. The first flash of lightning and the first boom of thunder were rousers, and as they were intent on watching the hay burn, the Indians were taken by surprise. They had not noticed the great thunderheads reaching high into the sky, and they had not seen the black crown of the shower as it followed down the Meduncook Valley. All at once they were soaked with rain, and so was the hay, and the fire went out.

There could be but one answer to anything like that. The Great Spirit was displeased with the Indians, and had shown his feelings with his thunderbolt. The Indians went away, and after a time the family came out to find the world peaceful, if soaked, and for once nobody complained that the hay got wet.

7

To straighten things out
concerning the amazing
Squantum, who was never
Squanto but was a trilingualist
and had some fun with the pious
Pilgrim Fathers when they
arrived, after long last, at
Plymouth, Maffachuffetts.

The importance of Squantum in Maine history has been damned by the faint whimsy of every historian in the libraries. There was one joker named Montgomery whose schoolday histories for the kiddies rammed the Big Pilgrim Myth down the throats of the generations. One of his better foolishments was how the Pilgrim Mothers founded washday. When the *Mayflower* got to Cape Cod, he wrote, the Pilgrim Mothers went ashore to do their laundry, and as this was on a Monday, Monday has been washday in New England ever since.

How can any teacher, assuming she is awake, pass that along to any student with a straight face and without the grain of salt? Don't teachers ever think about what they're teaching? The *Mayflower*, 120 gross tons, was no more than one of the vessels regularly fishing the Gulf of Maine from English ports. She wasn't much bigger than a Nova Scotia pinkie, although of a different shape. With 102 Pilgrims—men, women, and children—she took two months for the voyage, and carried not only supplies but the household effects for setting up housekeeping in America, i.e., grandfather clocks, Governor Winthrop desks, rocking chairs, cradles, and a considerable number of whatnots.

Now, does any good little boy or girl in the class want to raise a hand and tell us about the hygienic situation aboard the *Mayflower* when she arrived at Cape Cod? Let us not bother to recall that the sea had been less than calm and even bold Captain Standish had taken his daily turn at the rail. Let us not bother to reflect that the *Mayflower* had no inside plumbing. And so on and so forth. Just let us consider that 102 people had been cooped up in close company all the long route across the North Atlantic, from September 16 to November 21, 1620. Now, without impugning the piety and bravery and godliness of the good Pilgrims, does anybody in the class doubt that even Elder William Brewster needed a change of underwear? Come, come!

You bet the Pilgrim Mothers went ashore and did their washing, and not because it was Monday—they did their washing whatever day it was because they needed clean clothes.

Squantum has had about the same truthful treatment as washday. Montgomery was somewhat like General Custer—he couldn't tell one Indian from another. He kept getting Squantum mixed up with Samoset and Massosoit and Umbagoogie and Wampanoag and Narragansett and Charlie and Squanto, and some others. Squanto was a Saco Indian and had nothing to do with planting a hill of corn on a dead fish. (Not long ago some professor actually "researched" the dead fish story, attributing it to Squanto, and wrote a publish-or-perish treatise that got printed in a scientific journal!)

Well, here goes:

Squantum was never Squanto. Squanto came later. When Captain Jocelyn visited Maine and wrote his journal, he said that American Indians swam instinctively, and that a baby of but a few hours, if it fell in the water, would dog-paddle safely ashore. A few years after that, some Massachusetts militia were up along the Maine coast, and as they rowed a boat across the Saco River they came upon an Indian woman in a canoe. She had her baby with her. This was a wonderful chance to find out if Jocelyn had been right, so the men tipped the canoe over and learned that Jocelyn had been wrong. It happened that the squaw and her papoose belonged to Squanto, and while he had been friendly with the English up to that time, he now became very unfriendly indeed and grew mean and nasty. He perpetrated, or caused to be perpetrated, certain discourtesies of a revengeful nature which the English called "savage outrages," and because he accordingly became well-known he was frequently mistaken for Squantum.

Squantum's name was properly Tisquantum, and he was a sachem of the Pemaquid family of the Abnakis. The Pemaquids held a considerable hunting ground from the Kennebec River easterly past Meduncook and Muscongus, including the St. George River, but not quite to the Penobscot River. Later, in grants from the British Crown, the Pemaquid lands were called a "king-dom" and at another time were the "County of Cornwall." Pemaquid lay in what is now the town of Bristol. In Squantum's time Pemaquid was his home village. He was there in 1605 when Captain George Waymouth approached The Maine with the purpose of finding a suitable location for an English settlement. In his good ship *Archangel* Waymouth reached Monhegan Island, to which he was no stranger.

Captain Waymouth had been in command of a British gunboat for the past seventeen years, patrolling the English fisheries somewhat as our Coast Guard covers the same waters today. The historians who let you believe that nothing much was going on around here until the Pilgrims appeared are doing Captain Waymouth an injustice. He had many opportunities for various kinds of piracy and such, and as a consequence knew the coast from Carolina to Newfoundland the way any housewife knows her kitchen sink. Besides, all the Indians in the Pemaquid region had been paddling out to Monhegan Island every so often to sell furs and trade. So when Captain Waymouth appeared and his purpose was known, the Pemaquids took great interest in just what spot he would pick for his village-to-be. Squantum lost no time in approaching Waymouth, and they held powwow.

The kidnapping of five Pemaquid Indians by Waymouth, just before he returned to England, has been misplayed by the books. Some say the Indians were to be sold as slaves; others that they were to be exhibited like freaks in a circus. Not so. They were "kidnapped" as the only way to get them aboard the *Archangel* for the trip to England. They were not abused beyond being locked in, and after a few days at sea they accepted their lot and were given the run of the ship. Back in England three of them went to live in the household of Sir Ferdinando Gorges, the other two with His Lordship John Popham. Both men were corporators of the Plymouth Company; Popham was chief justice. Both lived at good addresses, and the Indians had the best of treatment in England.

The five Pemaquids were Nahanada, Skitwarroes, Assecomet, Tisquantum, and Dehamida. It was never meant that they would be exhibited, although the Indians seem to have had enough "ham" in them to make the most of their social appearances. Gorges wrote well of their manners and behavior. He also explained in his memoirs that capturing the Indians was his way of finding out what The Maine was like and to get their advice. There had been no intention of keeping them in England permanently, and Tisquantum was back at Pemaquid in 1606. There was no problem about his return trip; he came back on a vessel about to load fish at Monhegan Island.

Tisquantum, about to become Squantum, became a hero among his people, and if they'd had such things then, he would have gone to the Rotary Clubs to show his travel slides. And don't forget that he was also something of a hero in England, where he not only added greatly to his English but was able to use his French several times. He had learned French from a Jesuit missionary working among the Tontines. Squantum was a somebody.

It was the next year, 1607, in August, that the much-awaited Popham settlers arrived. The place for their settlement would be on the lower Sagadahock River, and it would be named Popham after His Lordship Sir John. Squantum was at home, relating his adventures in England once more to his children, and in comes Penelope, his number three squaw, to say, "Squantie, dear, the h'English 'as h'arrived." So no more had the first English foot trod the sterile and inhospitable sands of Popham Beach than up comes Squantum in a big canoe to welcome his friends!

There was hand shaking and backslapping, and messages from friends in England were delivered, and not a man (there were no women in the Popham company) was astonished that an American Indian could speak English. Squantum hesitated, but said that now he was here he might as well break bread, and in a few days he was a nuisance and everybody wished he'd go back to Pemaquid. But he had, indeed, uttered the historic "Welcome, Englishmen!" Those were to become his bywords.

Well, he sort of went on the circuit. He became a kind of official greeter and made a practice of going to welcome new arrivals and wish them well. In the years that followed he got down to Carolina, and he visited Newfoundland. Nobody in the United States ever knew it, but Squantum has his niche in Canadian history as he does in ours. In Labrador he was recognized as a Virginian.

Which brings us back to the Pilgrims, who have now come to Plymouth (a place Captain John Smith had shown on his map some years earlier) and Squantum is again in his tent at Pemaquid, lecturing again on his travels, and to him again comes Penelope to say, "Word comes, Squantie, that the Pilgrims have appeared." (She had somewhat improved her English in the meantime.)

"That so?" says Squantum. "I didn't know they'd left yet."

"Must have—they're here."

"Has their location been reported?"

"Ayeh. They're down in quahog country—Massachusetts. They got in Tuesday, after Monday washday."

"Wonder how many of 'em I know?" mused Squantum, and he arose to make wangan and set out for Plymouth (North Virginia).

So he appeared one morning, stepping from the woods, and Myles Standish looked up to say, "By the Old Harry, boys, here he comes now!" Everybody came to grasp Squantum's hand and pat him on the back, and then the Pilgrims all stood in a semicircle while Squantum cleared his throat and spoke the immortal words "Welcome, Englishmen!" Then they all had a good laugh, and gave Squantum the messages from the dukes and earls who remembered him from 1605.

Now comes the corn story. Squantum had lingered, and besides enjoying hospitality had been greatly amused at the curious notions and mannerisms of the Pilgrims. They wore funny hats, and carried their Bibles when they dug clams. And now Squantum told them to put a dead fish under each hill of corn. This is all right, and a dead fish under a hill of corn will fetch the crop along amazingly. The fish in context is the alewife, and squantum showed them how to dip alewives by the bushel when they came up the brooks with the tide. So the Pilgrims hoed an alewife under each hill of corn, and later that night Squantum bade his friends a fond farewell and headed back to Pemaquid. Squantum knew what was going to happen, and the Pilgrims didn't. It was the whimsy of Squantum to keep things to himself, and he chuckled like a good one all the way home.

Historians don't read too well, because the answer to this is in the journals of the Plymouth Colony. What happened is that the next night every raccoon, skunk, fox, bobcat, mink, fisher, otter, owl, pussycat, and lucivee in Massachusetts came to the Pilgrim gardens and dug up all the dead fish. Ha, ha, and ha. For a long time Squantum's recitation of this filled the tepees of the Pemaquids with jolly laughter. At Plymouth Governor John Winslow dutifully concluded the matter (if historians care to notice) with his journal entry: "Then they planted their gardens a second time and guarded them at night."

Squantum lived to be an old man, often visiting English settlements in fine British clothes made for him by Lord Popham's tailor, and affecting a gold-headed ebony walking stick in the manner of London dandies. He never went back to Plymouth, which explains why he lived to be an old man.

8

Possibly the first truthful historical account of the humiliating Battle of the Bagaduce, where Paul Revere did a good job but Commander Dudly Saltonstall made an ass of himself, which wasn't all that hard to do.

At the time of the American Revolution, not all the folks in Maine were in favor of rebellion. A decent proportion of the Mainers didn't feel, with the Adamses and the Hancocks, that they were being abused by His Majesty, and they weren't all heated up over port taxes and tea taxes and oppression and tyranny. There was one chap who got visited by the Committee on Public Safety and Correspondence, and while he was a Tory right enough, he made out. The world "Loyalist" came later.

These committees were supposed to seek out and take

care of Tories, and if you didn't hold up your hand and swear allegiance to the rebellion, you would be ridden about on a rail until you did. These committees were made up of upright Americans who were all for freedom and liberty and things like that. So the committee came to this chap and asked him if he believed in freedom, etc., and he told them that was his business and they should go climb a tree. At this, the committee sent out for the rail, but before it was brought in the chap's wife came with a pail of flip, and the meeting was recessed while everybody reasoned together. Soon after this informative incident, the Battle of the Bagaduce was fought, and one of the things to bear in mind is that our town of Castine was then mostly Tory.

The Bagaduce is a river that flows into the Penobscot by our Castine. The confluence was a strategic place to the original Indians, then to the French, later to what we'll call Mainers, and then in the revolution to the English. It became a base of operations against the colonies, supported by British installations at Halifax, and as aforesaid, the Tory population there helped things along. The fortifications and base at The Bagaduce had to be reduced, and about the time General George Washington was thawing his socks after his experiences at Valley Forge, Boston was fitting out a fleet to head east and take care of The Bagaduce.

It was quite a fleet. It had nineteen vessels with 328 guns, a thousand soldiers, and twenty-four transports with gear and supplies. The manifest included 1,200 gallons of rum and sufficient molasses to sweeten whatever flip, grog, and calibogus the expedition might require. The commander of this fleet was one Dudley Saltonstall, from a settled family much esteemed on Beacon Hill. Under him the soldiers were commanded by Brigadier General Solomon Lovell, and under him was Brigadier General Peleg Wadsworth. Peleg Wadsworth was to become the grandfather of the poet Henry Wadsworth Longfellow, who wrote "The Village Blacksmith," "The Psalm of Life," and "Paul Revere's Ride." In charge of the ordnance, which means the 328 cannon, was Lieutenant Colonel Paul Revere. The ships were sound, the soldiers eager and willing, Lovell was confident, Wadsworth and Revere were capable, and Saltonstall was a boob.

He was pompous and arrogant, officious in the extreme, and constantly aware that he was a gentlemen of the first water, blueblood and Brahmin, and that when he used the chamber mug it was just like strawberry shortcake. He brought the fleet to Sheepscot Bay to rendezvous, and the next morning—July 23, 1779—sailed for The Bagaduce, arriving off the British fortifications the next morning. The short pause at Boothbay Harbor pleased the chamber of commerce there, but it was a mistake—it allowed time for some Tory to get word to the English at The Bagaduce, and in turn for the English at The Bagaduce to send a messenger to Halifax. In short, Commander Saltonstall's arrival was expected.

Commander Saltonstall attacked on July 25. Colonel Revere plastered the English with a rousing cannonade, but an equally rousing westerly wind kept General Lovell from landing any men to follow up the barrage. This wind proved to be a "three-day blow," and everything waited for a flat-arse calm, which came the morning of the twenty-eighth. Colonel Revere repeated his bombardment, and boatloads of soldiers were sent in to land. But they had been sitting in the boats so long that they were muscle-bound and stiff, and they didn't jump about real spry. Besides, most of them had to go to the bathroom, so there was delay in forming platoons. Commander Saltonstall was annoyed.

But the sally was effective. Breaking ranks against orders, the men adjusted to the nature of the place and drove the English from their ramparts back into the main fort. Now was the time to unleash the dogs of war and give 'em hell, but Apostle Saltonstall held a big meeting with himself and decided on caution. Lovell and Wadsworth, and Colonel Revere, urged him to demand surrender at once and finish the job. The soldiers even drew up a petition asking him to stop dillying about, although not in that exact wording, and a committee approached the *Warren* and presented it. But Saltonstall was a boob, and said he thought perhaps he'd best send back to Boston for reinforcements. His action is not highly regarded at West Point and Annapolis, and while he piddled and diddled the English strengthened their defenses, and while they strengthened their defenses their relief was on its way from Halifax.

It got to be the thirteenth of August when General Lovell decided to risk insubordination and do something. He made a landing, and hoped Saltonstall would back him up with fire from the ships. We'll never know what Saltonstall decided, because just then the British rode up the Penobscot from Halifax with seven ships and 204 guns, 1,500 soldiers, and a bagpiper who was playing "An' owre the hill to Nanny, O!"

The disaster that followed was later closely considered by the General Court back in Boston. It plucked Apostle Saltonstall clean and forbade him ever again to hold any public position. The testimony at the trial showed that after the crew of his frigate *Warren* told him to swim for it and kicked him overboard, the men set fire to the *Warren* and thus kept her from falling into

British hands. At the same time, the General Court exonerated Generals Lovell and Wadsworth in all particulars, complimenting them on their conduct, and Lieutenant Colonel Paul Revere was awarded a beautiful silver bowl.

Thus the English were securely established on Penobscot Bay for the duration of the revolution. They were not too popular. At times they were nasty. If you weren't a Tory, they picked on you. One man, John Gilky, had five cows, and one day some British soldiers came and shot his five cows. This displeased Mr. Gilky, and quite a few Tories sympathized with him when they heard about it. Another man, Shubael Williams, was cutting wood one day and an English soldier walked up to him. The soldier had defected from the Castine fort and thought he'd like to become a colonial and take up a piece of land where he could raise chickens. Somehow, in escaping, he had lost his way. Shubael took him in and warmed him by his fire, gave him something to eat, and then put him on his way. Then the English caught this soldier and took him back to the fort, and then they came and tied Shubael to a tree. They laid on five hundred lashes to teach him that he shouldn't befriend an AWOL. Quite a few Tories in Castine regretted this, holding that a man who befriends a Redcoat can't be all wrong.

9

The proliferation of cruces along the Coast of Maine with the presumption these symbols of godliness would make people good, but also the details of how the Gotts hunted for hay thieves.

By the time the Pilgrims arrived at Plymouth, the coast of Maine looked like a military cemetery in Flanders. Between the crosses, row on row, small settlements were already practicing their ayeh's and thinking up insults for summer people. It had been the custom for everybody who came ashore in Maine to erect a cross and claim the land for some king or for his patron saint. Thorwald the Dane came first and put up two crosses and claimed Maine for Thor and Thoreau. In 1534 Jacques Cartier planted crosses and claimed everything south of the North Pole. De Monts planted a cross at Ste. Croix Island, but the soil was poor and he was a Huguenot and it didn't do well. Shortly Samuel Champlain arrived and doubled-crossed de Monts with a double-purpose cross and claimed everything for the Roman Catholic church.

Pring put up crosses. Gosnold put up crosses. John Smith put up crosses. The Guinness Book champion was Waymouth, who (quote) "put up a cross at every important point he touched at." Waymouth's historians don't tell us if the ship's carpenter made the crosses as needed, or if they towed a dory of British-made crosses behind the vessel. Waymouth's crosses superseded those of Champlain, because Waymouth had been a pirate for seventeen years before he came to Maine, and thus was Church of England. On Allen Island in the St. George River, the spot of one of Waymouth's crosses is known; in 1905, three hundred years after Waymouth, the Maine Historical Society put up a handsome granite cross that cost a bundle and can still be seen. Allen Island is in the town of St. George.

Since so many crosses went up along the coast of Maine, we could presume the early settlers were a pious lot and far more devout than the Bostonians. As we have seen, this would be an erroneous presumption. It appears the prevalence of these Christian symbols had little salutary effect. For instance, Fathers Biard and Massé dutifully erected a cross near St. Sauveur, to propitiate that community, and almost in the shadow of that cross a wonderful but inappropriate event came to pass which is worth our attention.

A settlement had come about, some years after St. Sauveur had been eliminated by Captain Samuel Argal, and along the shore by this settlement was a tidal flat to be known at Pretty Marsh. Beauty had nothing to do with the name—it comes from the Mainer's use of "pretty" for considerable. One settler said to another,

"Pretty marshy out there!" The other man said, "Ayeh, tha's right—pretty marshy."

Being marshy, the flat was not of a kind suited to clams, but it did grow a wealth of hay—salt hay, or "saltay." This saltay was by no means as good to feed out as prime meadow hay, but it was still a lush crop, and under the rule of waste-not-want-not the settlers used it. Since the flats didn't belong to anybody but were common property, each man cut as he pleased and what he cut was his.

This hay required "staddles." A staddle is a platform made by driving stakes into the mud in a circular pattern, so the hay will keep dry on the elevation, the staddle being tall enough to let the tide come and go below its level. So a man would cut his saltay and arrange it on his staddles, and it would be there when he needed it for his cattle. A stack of saltay on a staddle looks something like a big mushroom. When saltay can be had for the cutting, there is no great reason to steal any, but at Pretty Marsh this came about. All at once a staddle was empty, and a stack of saltay gone. Then another stack disappeared, and while nobody much cared where the hay went, everybody was curious as to who took it. During the second season more saltay disappeared, and although everybody kept watch, nobody saw anybody take any.

Along about this time the folks down in Boston began looking at Maine as an attractive piece of property. France and England kept pointing at their numerous crosses of discovery and claiming ownership, but affairs in Europe occupied royal attention, and matters in the colonies were ignored. Boston was handier and took advantage. Overtures were made to woo the Mainers, and the puzzled settlers near Pretty Marsh took advantage. Somebody said, "If Massachusetts is so interested in us, let 'em find out who the hell is stealing our saltay!" So they sent down a petition asking the general court at Boston to make an appropriation and investigate the thievery. Most of the settlers who signed the petition lived on Mount Desert Island proper, and in the vicinity of Pretty Marsh: Abe Somes, Andy Tarr, Jim, Steve, Tom, and Elijah Richardson, and Ben Stanwood. But three other settlers who signed the petition were from Gott's Island— offshore and for five thousand years the winter quarters for aboriginal Maine people. The three were Steve, Dan, and Dan Gott, Jr., who were illustrious forebears of generations of stout Maine men anybody would be proud to claim.

Steve and the two Dans had come ashore to lament this lawless heisting of hay, and joined in the general perplexity as to who might be the criminal. What are things coming to, anyway? Yes—they'd be glad to sign the petition. In Boston there was some hilarity over stealing salt hay, but the General Court wanted to keep the Mainers happy, deplored the thievery, and raised some money to investigate. When news of this appropriation came to the folks by Pretty Marsh, the three Gotts generously offered to serve as watchmen and vigilantes, and, receiving the authority and the appropriation, they went to work. They never caught anybody. During several seasons they mounted watch and chased down all clues. But in spite of the Gotts, hay continued to disappear, and the saltay thieves of Pretty Marsh were never apprehended.

And all of this right in the shadow of the cross!

It took a week, but seldom much more, to run a sloop from Gott's Island to Boston and back. Boston was not only a good market for edible salt hay, but it had other uses there besides feeding animals. It made packing in crates and barrels for pottery, and also for bottles of rum. Some was used in burning bricks. A big use was for mats aboard vessel, straw fenders against bumping another ship or a wharf. After several years the General Court at Boston withdrew its support for apprehending the Pretty Marsh hay thieves, but the Gott boys said the money was no object and they would continue the search as a public service. They said they were happy to be of use, even if unpaid. The other settlers extended a vote of thanks to them for this kindness. Nobody until now ever imagined the Gotts were working both sides of the salt hay business.

10

What happened at Fort St. George on the twenty-second day of June, 1814, including the threat by Ephraim Wylie to the British marines that if they didn't go away and leave him be, he'd set his dog on them.

The War of 1812—Mr. Madison's War—ruined the maritime trade in which Maine shipbuilders, Maine sea captains, and Maine investors were so heavily involved, so there were plenty of Mainers who weren't all that happy about it. You'll find that every history book has a detailed account of the big naval battle between the English *Boxer* and our *Enterprise*, a spectacular fight which our *Enterprise* won—if anybody ever wins a thing like that. That battle took place in the open ocean near Monhegan Island on September 5, 1814, just a few miles from the place on the St. George River where a far more spectacular battle had taken place going on three months earlier. Reference is to the English attack on Fort St. George.

The list of vessels built in Thomaston and the town's roster of seafarers, plus a long tradition of commerce, were good reasons for a fort down the river to protect our interests there. It wasn't all that much of a fort. Shaped half-moon, it had ramparts looking out on the St. George River, and its three eighteen-pounder guns were considered adequate to deter any enemy that might come sailing up the river to despoil Thomaston. There were barracks for the militia stationed there, a block-house, and a powder room. The position was strategic, and all had been made ready several years before the War of 1812 broke out.

But as the war approached, the defense of Thomaston seemed less important than some other tactics, and the militia had been transferred to other places, leaving Fort St. George empty and forlorn. By the time the war started, Fort St. George was in charge of a civilian of the Town of St. George, one Hezekiah Prince, who was paid a small fee to keep his eye on the place. He, in turn, hired a gentleman named Ephraim Wylie to do the actual caretaking, and to live at the fort. Mr. Wylie was aged. He was otherwise unoccupied, and a man of quiet habit who would not mind being alone. With his dog and his cat he had lived at Fort St. George since the militia had left, and he was content.

The day of the big battle at Fort St. George was June 22, 1814.

Unbeknownst to Ephraim Wylie, the British navy had given orders to the commanding officer of HMS *Bulwark*, a seventy-four-gun ship of the line, to proceed up the St. George River, reduce Fort St. George, and sack the town of Thomaston. The *Bulwark* was, accordingly, soon off Monhegan Island and ready for action. But a clinging thick-o'-fog settled in on a sticky southerly whisper of air, and the commander of the *Bulwark* wisely decided to delay his approach to the St. George River until he could at least see his hand before his face. He dropped anchor to wait things out.

But a pea-souper that will put the British navy out of business isn't about to hinder a Mainer when he has something to do, and a venturesome resident of Thomaston decided this would be a fine time to take a cargo of lime to Boston. Movements of lime to Boston hadn't been too frequent of late, the way the British were patrolling our coast, and a good fog was a blessing. So Rupert Slater cast off and drifted with the current down the St. George River, a course he knew by heart and could follow in his sleep, and shortly he lifted a sail and caught what slight air there was—and lo! he was on his way to Boston with fifty tons of lime.

Next thing he knew he cussid-near whacked into the side of a hulkin' great warship anchored right in the channel. The master of the *Bulwark* regarded this as fortunate, and with a pistol at his ear our friend Rupert Slater agreed to pilot the *Bulwark* upriver to Fort St. George and Thomaston. It seemed the sensible thing to do. Besides, the commanding officer told Rupert that if he did this, he could get his lime boat back and have a free ticket to Boston. Fair enough, if you look at it this way.

The British marines thus arrived at Fort St. George, landing on the shore below and marching up the hill in the fog. They naturally expected their appearance would be a surprise to the defenders of the place. This proved to be true. Ephraim Wylie was, at the moment, making his lunch, and was having a bit of trouble getting his fire to flame up. His cat was asleep on his bed-bunk, and his dog, who was stone deaf, was asleep behind the wood box. Mr. Wylie frequently talked to himself in his lonesomeness, and he was doing this now—by times replying to his own remarks. He was annoyed to hear, just as his fire seemed promising, footsteps on his rampart, and said to himself that this was no time to have company show up.

The officer of the British marines had not expected to get onto the rampart without some resistance from the fort—his intelligence had been faulty, and he didn't know that the militia had been removed years ago and Mr. Wylie was in residence. So, suspicious of a trap, he ordered his marines to stand back, and he boomed out an order for the fort to capitulate and all hands to surrender to His Majesty. Mr. Wylie did not respond.

The officer of the marines now ordered a shot at the door. The musket ball ripped through, just missed Mr. Wylie, and hit the bunk, whereat the cat went up the wall. Mr. Wylie was a kindly man and fond of his cat, so now he went to the door, pushed it open, and ordered the marines off. "You're trespassing!" he shouted. He said if they didn't leave, he'd set his dog on them.

Since things were so, the officer of the marines had the three eighteen-pounders spiked, and then withdrew his men to the vessel and kept on going upstream to sack Thomaston. Meantime, Mr. Wylie prepared his lunch and ate it. And with Rupert Slater as pilot, the British soon came to the downstream outskirts of Thomaston and set a house afire. This attracted the attention of a certain Captain Gilchrist, who surmised a blaze of that sort could have been started only by a British attack, and he grabbed up a fowling piece he had loaded with goose shot and fired it blindly into the fog on the off chance he might connect. When his gun went off, the noise alerted several citizens over across on the Cushing side of the river, and they came down and began shooting at Captain Gilchrist. This volley was heard downriver, below Fort St. George, by a couple of boys who had a swivel gun, and they made answer.

By this time Mr. Wylie, in Fort St. George, had finished his lunch, and had gone out to remove the spikes from his three eighteen-pounders and to load the cannon just in case those blasted Britishers came back, damn 'em! And, upon hearing the swivel gun, he touched off his three cannon.

The British officer, completely lost in the fog, and not all that trustful of Rupert Slater, concluded from the noise that he was surrounded and outnumbered, and prudently pushed off down the river to safety. Thus Fort St. George saved the Town of Thomaston from rapine and pillage, Ephraim Wylie became a hero of the War of 1812, and, redeeming his vessel for services rendered, Rupert Slater made a safe voyage to Boston and sold his fifty tons of lime.

I I

A sketch of the great
Prohibitionist, Neal Dow, and
some instances of his influence on
his fellow State-o'-Mainers,
causing some of them to stoop to
various iniquities inconsistent
with the usual righteousness.

No other state has ever offered a combination of pious
iniquity to equal that of Neal Dow of Maine. He was a
good-looking fellow. He was the "Father of Prohibition" and was known in his time all over the world for
his unrelenting fight against John Barleycorn and Demon
Rum and their numerous henchmen. It was he who
brought to Maine its most prosperous era, the era of the
bootlegger, the rumrunner, and the scofflaw—an era of
great wealth and derring-do, an era of wealth not matched
even by the blue-water sea captains of the windjammers
or the timberland barons of the North Woods. It was

an era famous for "drinking wet and voting dry," and in his day Neal Dow believed sincerely that Franklin Delano Roosevelt would never amount to anything.

Neal Dow was born and died in Portland, and during his life traveled the world over to promote prohibition. He did not, as a child, embrace the general Maine passion for flip. And he *was* a bright, keen, eager youngster of the Frank Merriwell stripe, facile in mind and able at athletics. When scarce a tot he could swim like a fish, and saved two men from drowning, but not at the same time. He could shoot, run, fence, sail, and was handy with his fists—but he did all those things only in self-defense and was never dirty or mean. All Portland schoolchildren are required to memorize the story of Neal Dow and the monkey:

There was a man who kept a monkey, or some kind of baboon or gibbon, behind the fence in his dooryard to keep the boys out. The beast was fierce. This man used to taunt the boys and dare them to come in and see what the monkey would do to them. Young Dow, then too young to realize what he was doing, took the dare and went in like David to handle Goliath. Young Dow did get some scratches and he had his clothes torn off, but he whopped the monkey some old good. In much the same way, Neal Dow was to tackle alcohol and cause it to cower.

He was born in 1804, and served as mayor of Portland from 1851 to 1858. He was dignified, learned, and always a gentleman. Two Portland streets are named for him—Neal Street and Dow Street. (William Street, Pitt Street, and Fessenden Street are named for William Pitt Fessenden.) It was in 1851 that Neal Dow succeeded in getting his "Maine Law" passed at Augusta, thus making Maine "dry" in every respect except drinking. It was the pattern for similar laws in other states, and was to remain in force until FDR got the Eighteenth Amendment to the United States Constitution repealed in 1933. When that Eighteenth Amendment was ratified as a consequence of Neal Dow's efforts, it brought upon Maine the aforesaid era of the bootlegger.

There was nothing otherwise frivolous in Dow's career. As a young man he was an engineer in the Portland Fire Department. After one particular fire he cited one of his firemen for insubordination. The fireman said he had been ordered by Dow to perform something that was idiotic, foolish, impossible, and extremely dangerous. But he did admit that after he refused, Dow went ahead and did it. Another time, when Dow was mayor, he tried to go to his office in the city hall, and found his way blocked by four policemen who were being held at bay by a kook with a pistol. Dow walked up to the kook, took his gun away, and passed it to one of the policemen as he continued on to his office. Another time some tavern keepers hired a ruffian off a ship to beat Dow up as he was going to a temperance meeting, and Dow left him whimpering in the street.

His skill as an orator will explain his success with his efforts to get his prohibition bill passed. One evening he was to lecture on the evils of drink at the Portland City Auditorium, and his reputation as a speaker turned out a huge crowd. People came in the afternoon to stand in line. The main hall and the corridors were jammed, and people stood in the streets. The result was that when Dow arrived to speak he couldn't get in.

After the Maine Law was enacted, Dow went to other countries to urge prohibition, and was a success everywhere except in Scotland. Although considered overage, Dow offered himself for Civil War duty, and was given a colonel's command in the Thirteenth Maine Regiment of Volunteers. He rose to be brigadier general and in action proved a competent officer. His dedication to temperance gave President Abraham Lincoln an opportunity for a pleasantry. When the little old lady told President Lincoln that General Grant drank whiskey, President Lincoln said, "Find out what kind and I'll get some for all my other generals—except Neal Dow." Dow was wounded twice at the battle of Port Hudson, once in an arm and once in a leg.

But for all his efforts, Maine never became as parched as he wanted. One legendary remark goes, "The best drink I ever had in Maine was in Berlin, New Hampshire." Canada, as well, and the West Indies and the other cider mills were too close. Then, the Maine Law made exceptions for spirits that would be used for medicinal, mechanical, and artistic purposes. This made everybody an artist or mechanic, except those who had good doctors. Apothecaries were much esteemed.

When the Eighteenth Amendment did go into effect, forcing the whole United States into the same predicament, Maine had the jump on all the other states by reason of experience—we had been living with it since 1851. We knew just what to do. Through the 1920s, Maine had the same thing as a license to steal. Those who didn't have boats to bring liquor ashore had trails through the woods to Canada. The icehouse at every sporting camp in Maine had its cache in the sawdust and a choreboy who knew just where to dig to find the gin and the scotch. Every cove became a Smugglers' Cove, and not every lobster boat was hauling lobsters. "Mother" boats would jog outside the three-mile limit ready to hand down square five-gallon cans to authorized applicants. The Volstead agents, meant to enforce prohibition, didn't have much luck catching Maine fishermen in their own waters, or Maine guides in their own woods. A few remembered incidents will show what Neal Dow did for Maine:

A gentleman sound asleep in his bed heard a midnight commotion in his dooryard and looked out to see a truck in the moonlight. He pulled on his pants and slippers and stepped out onto his back piazza, which gave on the salt water. As he stuck it out, his nose fitted into the muzzle of a shotgun, and a rude voice told him he would be smart to go back to bed and forget what he saw. He did so, and what he saw was a boat that was unloading square cans and a bunch of men loading them into the truck. In the morning he was pleased to find one of the square cans on his back piazza, with a note attached that said "Thank you."

Then one night Ralph Goodenow had 138 gallons of King William scotch under the back seat of his Hudson Supersix, and it was his purpose to deliver them to a man who would be waiting in the cemetery at Locke's Mills at 3:00 A.M. Then he noticed that he was being overtaken by a vehicle which he surmised would be that of a sheriff. Mr. Goodenow increased his speed, and a chase ensued that would cover many roads and many miles that Mr. Goodenow had never seen before. He did elude the sheriff all right, but now he didn't know where he was and he was low on gasoline. He was surprised, and delighted, to come around a curve and see a gasoline pump with the lights on at that hour, so he pulled in. A woman came out in a bathrobe and filled his tank. In those days five gallons of gasoline and a quart of oil would cost ninety-five cents, and now Mr. Goodenow handed the woman a twenty-dollar bill. "Gracious," she said. "I can't change that, but my husband can. He's just come home—he's been out all night chasing a bootlegger!" Mr. Goodenow said, "Keep the change," and went his way.

Once a sheriff caught a boat unloading square cans, and he "seized" the liquor and put it in a truck to go to the police station as evidence. The driver of the truck started up, and the sheriff stood with the load in the back of the truck to guard it in transit. At every utility pole along the road, the sheriff tossed off a square can in such a manner that he could find it again. At the police station the quantity of evidence was diminished, but nobody stood up and shouted about that. When the sheriff retraced the route to pick up the rest of the evidence, he was sorry to find the driver of the truck had retraced it before he did.

Thus a certain depravity of morals was visited upon Maine people by Neal Dow's Maine Law, and it got so you couldn't really trust anybody. There was a devout Baptist minister in a town suburban to Portland who went three mornings a week to visit his parishioners who were patients at the State Street Hospital. He had a Model T touring car, with fold-back top and side curtains, so he could make this trip in any weather, and consequently was reliable. He would park his vehicle and step into the hospital, and almost at once a certain Mr. Geoffrey Hoskins would stroll up State Street from the direction of the waterfront. He would pause and insert a brown paper bag in the back of the minister's automobile, and then he would continue his stroll leisurely up State Street towards Congress Square.

When the minister had visited all his parishioners, he would come from the hospital, crank his car, and get behind the wheel and go home. But it was his custom, when he arrived in his hometown, to go into the post office to get his mail and to go into the variety store and pick up a newspaper. This allowed ample time for Mr. Danforth P. Swerringon to walk by and pick up the brown paper bag, and contents, that Mr. Geoffrey Hoskins had placed in the automobile. In short, these two evil companions had made an unwitting rumrunner of the good minister. We should all shudder at the infinite injustice if the Volstead agents had arrested the minister and taken him before the judge. The incident serves to show how Maine people were corrupted by the good intentions of Neal Dow.

Even federal officers! A lady coming into Maine from Quebec put a pint of whiskey in her "budge" to conceal it from the customs officer. As she braked to stop for customs inspection, momentum thrust her against the steering wheel and the bottle was broken. When the agent leaned down to speak to her through the window, the rich flavor engulfed him. He recognized the aroma, and the lady decided the best way out was to tell the truth, and she began picking glass out of her shirt. At this, the customs officer said, "Oh, that's too bad—wait a minute and I'll get you a replacement." She thus received a bottle he had taken from a tourist who hadn't been so honest—or so good-looking.

And the lesser constabulary! An elderly lady was told by her doctor to have regular alcohol rubdowns, and she found that lawful alcohol on prescription from the pharmacist was expensive. So she spoke to the county sheriff, and for years he kept her supplied with top-grade alcohol at a much cheaper price—he took it from the "evidence" locked up in the courthouse basement, five gallons at a time.

It was, in short, outrageous the way Neal Dow's prohibition movement seduced the good and honest people of the State of Maine and made a mockery of their inherent righteousness.

General Neal Dow retained his health and vigor, and his mental acumen, into his nineties, and attributed his longevity to his regular habits, abstinence from liquor and tobacco, exercise, caution at table, and sparing sociability with the fair sex. And retiring at early hours. It has been said that he really didn't live into his nineties—that with his numerous abstinences it just seemed that long.

12

Continuing the study of the effect of Neal Dow on the otherwise law-abiding State-o'-Mainer and some remarks about William B. Edwards, chief of police in Brunswick, who hated liquor and enforced the prohibition law.

Neal Dow died in Portland in 1897, so he didn't live to see the budding iniquities of his temperance movement burst into the magnificent depravities rampant in Maine after the Eighteenth Amendment took effect in 1920. The "Prohibition Era" was the Golden Age of the Scofflaw, and Maine eagerly embraced the prosperity of the bootlegger and rumrunner. The coast of Maine was too big and the number of revenuers too few, and rewards were juicy. The way corruption worked, it was often kind and generous. Billy Edwards used to work very closely with Ralph M. Ingalls, who was a respectable lawyer in Portland.

Billy Edwards was incorruptible. Born William B. Edwards, he was the son of the minister at the Growstown Church in Brunswick, a cocky kid but a good student. Although short, he took no guff from bigger boys, and he developed an ability to strut sitting down. He grew up to be a professional public servant for Brunswick, and in his time held every office except president of Bowdoin College and master of the Masonic Lodge. He shone as chiefs of the police department and the fire department, simultaneously, but was also selectman, overseer of the poor, dog officer, plumbing inspector, probation officer, bail commissioner, janitor of the town hall, sealer of weights and measures, truant officer, deputy sheriff, humane officer, milk inspector, weigher of hay and scaler of wood, bark, and lumber, and he ran up the flag every morning and took it down at night. During an unforeseen emergency, he substituted as police matron.

In his class Maine never had any other person who even approached Billy. He was a keen detective, and had an "informant" system so effective that he often knew about crimes before they happened. County, state, and even federal officers would throw their hands in the air, and then Billy would solve the mystery and make an arrest. He never studied law, but his frequent appearances in Brunswick Municipal Court as prosecutor made him competent, and few attorneys in Maine looked forward to defending against him. Nothing herein should be construed as negative about Billy Edwards—he was a great man of almost universal talents, vigorous and dedicated, honest as the day is long. His heart was in the right place, and he was compassionate. He hated liquor and he hated rumrunners, and his jurisdiction was just about the only one where the scofflaw stayed uncomfortable.

As a boy, influenced by his reverend father, Billy had "signed the pledge," promising to look not upon the wine when it was red. Thou shouldst not take a fellow nine years old and make him swear to never kiss the girls, but with Billy the pledge worked. He never tasted liquor, detested it and its adherents, and this explains his dedicated vigilance in pursing Brunswick rumrunners when prohibition became the law. When Billy was old and had ceased all his numerous public duties, he was in constant pain and faced a lingering end. Dr. Richardson, who had the Brunswick Hospital, felt the distraction of an ounce or two of whiskey might ease Billy's discomfort, and prescribed. Billy, somehow suspecting this, put up a fuss and would have none of it. "Doctor's orders!" said Dr. Richardson, but Billy clenched his teeth and held to his boyhood pledge unto death.

Billy's prohibition beat was the coastline of eastern Casco Bay, with coves and inlets perfect for smuggling. That coastline was also the home-haunt of some of the best lobstermen in the business. The lobstermen readily embraced their inheritance from Neal Dow, and had a certain native immunity—Billy saw no point in going after boats when the culprit was liquor. So the lobstermen would go beyond the three-mile limit, where a "mother ship" would be jogging, and upon proper application would receive square five-gallon cans of stuff "right off the boat." On shore somewhere, a truck from Cranston, Rhode Island, would be waiting for a lobsterman to touch base, and by the time an enforcement officer, even Billy, could arrive, the truck would be well on its way and the lobsterman home in bed, where his wife was ready to swear that he hadn't been out of the house since noon. There is reason to believe that there were "cahoots" about this, and that enforcement officers could be persuaded to hunt in the wrong places.

But not with Billy Edwards. Billy was, far and away, the only enforcement officer in Maine, at any level, who meant business. It wasn't every landing that he knew about, and only now and then would he connect. But when he got a "tip," the jig was up. The booze he seized would be trucked to the Brunswick police station, and the rumrunners he arrested photographed and booked. It was the custom of the "syndicate" to send only clean men on these trucking errands to Maine. Accordingly, Billy never arrested a rumrunner with a record. Once a rumrunner got a record, he was never sent to Maine again. So those that Billy arrested were readily eligible for bail, and once cash bail was posted, they left Maine and that was that. The simple routine of posting bail frustrated Billy Edwards.

Well, when a successful raid was in progress and the liquor and the rumrunners were on their way to the police station, Billy would arrive to find the respectable lawyer from Portland, Attorney Ralph M. Ingalls, waiting for him. It wasn't always Ingalls, but it was most of the time. Since Portland is twenty-five miles from Brunswick, and the total possible elapsed time might be fifteen minutes, there seemed a tinge of conspiracy in this. Besides, Attorney Ingalls would have a briefcase full of money still in its bank wrappers, and he would have the bail papers all filled out by typewriter, and it was usually just about 2:30 A.M. Also, Attorney Ingalls would be fully dressed, as if on his way to plea before the Supreme Court, and he would even have a stickpin in his necktie. Billy Edwards could never in conscience condone what he suspected, but in Maine the people had been long conditioned to the peculiar morality of the Neal Dow casuistry, and not even Billy was astonished when Attorney Ingalls was afterward elected county attorney and honored by the bar association.

13

Even those who moved back from the ocean had the sea in their hearts, and loved their boats. How Jacob Eaton tried to be a miller but didn't like it, and drowned himself at St. John. A tale of West Farmington.

The shipbuilding that went on along the Maine coast in the great days of deep-water sail has been adequately chronicled, and it is a big story. From Kittery to Calais, the stroke of the adze and the reeling of the calking mallet were symphony to Maine's prosperity, but this music to the attentive ear wasn't limited to tidewater and the estuaries. Mainers built boats back in the highlands, and it was nothing for coastal folks to look up on a pleasant morning and see some farmer teaming his oxen down from the mountain, bringing his new boat sedately along in its cradle to have a "la'nch." There are good records, although incomplete, of the boatyards and shipyards of Maine coastal towns, coves, inlets, and even eelruts, but not so much was set down about craft built in up-country barns.

Or parlors. Many tales persist of boats that were built in houses, often far back from the ocean, and how a man would take down the front of his home to get his boat out. These tales are repeated as if the man were a mite odd and should have known better, like a painter who brushes himself into a corner. It was not really so. These rational people, driven by the urge to build a boat, knew from the beginning they would have to take down a wall. That was no great chore. Finish the boat, put a forenoon into removing the wall, and after the boat is out another forenoon to put things back.

Mellie Collins, a master sloop builder of Freeport, would turn out a beautiful sloop almost every winter, making her right in his front room so people passing could look in the window to see the progress, and as regularly his front wall would come down and go up again. Mellie lived a good mile from any ocean. But Satchell-Eye Dyer, who lived in Bowdoin, had a better way. When he built his first boat in his parlor, he took down the wall, removed the boat, and then hung the wall back on hinges, all ready for his next boat. Then he'd prop the wall up on two posts and back in his steers. And doing carpenter work in a parlor is no joke, either. Every home had a parlor, but it was seldom used as such. For funerals, and if the minister called in summer. Families lived in heated kitchens in the winter. So the parlor was there, and it was perfect for a boat shop. When Satchell-Eye Dyer died his family cleaned out the shavings and held his funeral, and then the front wall was propped up and the hearse was backed right in.

There was at least one man, name of Reddin, who lived back a few miles, and he brought his lumber down to the shore and built his boat right where he could launch her. It was on the lawn of the minister, the Rev. Thomas Smith, right on Clay Cove at Portland. The parson kept a diary, and he jotted down the progress on the boat every day, so we have a good record, right up to the launch.

Maybe the best up-country boat story is that of Jacob Eaton of Farmington, a town far up from the sea, in the valley of the Sandy River. Mr. Eaton had been born on the coast, but like a lot of coastal folks in the late 1700s he moved to the highlands to find a new prosperity on the land. Fact is that many of these folks were weary of the coast and the sea and wanted to leave it far behind. Not far from Mr. Eaton's Farmington, just over the hill in the Carrabasset Valley, a settlement at New Vineyard had been made by several families from Martha's Vineyard, in Massachusetts Bay. They moved because they had suffered too much from Dat Ol' Debbil Sea. Too many boats lost at sea, too many husbands and sons drowned, and there had been too much sea fog and drizzle and mist and other variations of coastal weather. If you know where to look, you can still find the cellar holes of their pioneer homes—deep in the woods and high on a hill. They certainly did get away from the ocean.

So Jacob Eaton became partner in a mill which may have been the first of its kind in that part of Maine. With a dam and a wheel on a tributary of Sandy River, they were ready to saw lumber and to grind grain, and were on their way to prosperity when the "bug" hit

Jacob. All at once he came down with a feverish yen to make himself a boat and go back to sea. He built his boat just upriver from present Farmington, on the way to Strong, and the route to his ocean was down Sandy River, into the Kennebec above Norridgewock, down the Kennebec until it joined the Androscoggin at Merrymeeting Bay, and then the length of what was then called the Sagadahock River to the open sea. If Jacob Eaton, while he was making his boat, chanced to sing "I must down to the seas again," he wasn't just flapping his lips. Then he launched his boat below the mill dam, worked her down, all the way down, and he took her to sea. So it was with the jolly life of the miller in West Farmington, one hand on the hopper and the other on the sack.

Jacob was happy to be back at sea, and for a time he prospered with his boat as he traded up and down the coast. But then disaster struck. He was in St. John harbor when he misjudged the Fundy tide. The highest tides in the world plague seamen in the Bay of Fundy, and the St. John River as it flows into the harbor at St. John is a boobytrap to the inexperienced and unwary. As the river reaches the harbor it forms a "reversing falls"—the river flows toward the sea with strength and as it meets the fierce tidal flood the maelstrom forms. Jacob zigged when he should have zagged, and his boat went under—cargo and Jacob and all. Today tourists stand on the bridge there and gaze down in awe at the oddity of the reversing falls, and if they knew anything about Jacob Eaton they would readily understand how he came to his end there—so very far from West Farmington.

His tragedy did not, however, warn Mainers and deter them from building boats and going to sea.

14

The Greenback Movement, and
how the State of Maine came to
have five, six, and maybe seven
governors all at once, and how
old Solon Chase used to wave his
goadstick and yell, "Lookit them
steers!"

The age-old reputation of the Down-Mainer for canny,
homespun, reliable, inherent, unequaled intelligence is
excessively gratuitous, for he can be the biggest dam-
phool most of the time, and when he goes to vote he
usually is. The best example of this native knack for
stupidity came back in the year 1879, when he embraced
the so-called Greenback Movement and really let himself go. No other state has ever put on such a circus of
absurdity, and probably none ever will—but there's
no assurance whatever that the canny, etc., State-o'-

Mainer won't repeat the thing any day now, and probably do better on the next time around.

During the Civil War money took a beating. Both the
Union and the Confederate states handled their finances
with "fiat" money. That is, there was no backing of the
paper dollar with gold or silver, and all the people could
count on was the integrity of the government to live up
to its obligations. Confederate money went sour and
down the drain, and the Union dollar had its bad
moments. Mostly because of a Maine man, Hugh
McCulloch, who was secretary of the Treasury, the
Union dollar recovered and stability returned—the North
went back to "specie." That was called "hard money"—
backed by gold, silver, and government securities.
Interesting that during that period three Mainers were
secretaries of the Treasury—McCulloch, William Pitt
Fessenden, and Lot Morrill, three sturdy believers in
hard money. But before fiscal stability could be brought
about, there arose the "Greenback Party"—made up of
nuts who thought the government should just print
enough paper money so everybody could have all he
wanted, without any heed to what the money was worth.
The dollar bill was a greenback in current slang, and
the Greenbackers wanted to keep printing greenbacks
until everybody was rich. The Greenback philosophy
petered out in the rest of the country before the canny
Down-Mainers embraced it on the ebb tide. The
Greenback Party first got prominent in Maine in the
election of 1878.

At that time our governor and legislature were elected
for one-year terms, and the governor had to get a majority of the votes cast. If no candidate for governor got a
majority, the election was thrown into the House of

Representatives and the members made a choice. The Democrat candidate in 1878 was Dr. Alonzo Garcelon of Lewiston, and because so many Democrats had embraced Greenbackism (plus a few Republicans) he didn't get a majority. So the legislators named Garcelon governor, and after his year in office he announced that the wouldn't run again. A good guess would be that he foresaw some heavy weather breeding and decided to be smart.

If so, he was right, because the election of 1879 was a derry-down dandy. Even today, it's hard to tell if Maine elected five or maybe six, and possibly seven, governors, or whatever they were. Certainly there was good cause to doubt the canny intelligence of the native stock. Things went somewhat like this:

Since none of the three candidates for governor— Republican, Democrat, Greenback—gained a majority, the legislature made ready to act again. On the face of the returns, the Republicans had a majority of the legislators, which would mean a Republican governor. But at this point Governor Garcelon, still in office, had a brilliant idea. He and his Democrat council would be the "returning board" for the elections; here was a chance to certify the elections in such way that the Democrats won the House and could elect a Democrat governor. His strategy was called the "Count Out."

Local ballot clerks do the best they can, but any election, anywhere, has its little errors. Usually, corrections can be made and no harm done. Maybe only two of the three selectmen signed the warrant. Perhaps a clock was wrong and the polls closed ten minutes late. Governor Garcelon now seized on such technicalities and began "counting out" Republicans who had already been, so to speak, elected. Mistakes were uncovered that might have counted out Democrats and Greenbacks, but corrections were permitted and no Democrats and no Greenbacks got counted out. By the time Governor Garcelon and his Democrat council "certified" the election results, Maine had a "Fusionist" legislature—Democrats and Greenbacks joining to make life miserable for the Republicans.

This matter did, indeed, go to the Supreme Court, which decided (rightly) against Garcelon, and a Republican House did elect Republican Daniel F. Davis governor, who qualified and served. Perhaps we should take notice that the Supreme Court had but one Democrat justice, but we should also observe that he couldn't swallow the Garcelon device and the decision was unanimous.

But while the Supreme Court was taking its time to examine the evidence and arrive at a decision, Governor Garcelon remained in office after his term expired on the palpable grounds that his successor had not been named and he had not been lawfully replaced. Garcelon thus became Maine's Governor No. 1 in the year 1880.

When the new legislature convened, with the right people counted in, the Senate had eleven Republicans and twenty Fusionists. The House had sixty-one Republicans and seventy-eight Fusionists. The Republicans in both houses offered a number of motions, all of which were defeated, and then the fun began. The Senate organized and elected James D. Lamson of Waldo County as its president, the Republican members abstaining. Since the Constitution of the State of Maine makes the President of the Senate next in line to the Governor, Lamson thus was considered to be the governor, but he modestly held himself back and didn't presume to insist. However, he would be Governor No.

2 in the year 1880, give or take as necessary. At least he held himself in readiness.

By now Governor Garcelon mistrusted he had erred somehow, and he longed to return to private practice, and wished he could, and when he couldn't convince good old Jim Lamson to take over, he proclaimed a public emergency and named General Joshua L. Chamberlain Military Governor to keep the peace and protect the state until the rightful governor could be found. Chamberlain, the hero of Little Round Top at Gettysburg, had already been a duly elected governor in 1867, was as popular as rum and gin throughout Maine, and everybody was glad for this choice. Everybody liked the general. He mounted cannon on the statehouse steps and asked everybody to stay calm. And General Joshua L. Chamberlain thus became Maine's Governor No. 3 in the year 1880.

But now Jim Lamson saw things had changed. Dr. Garcelon would step down, leaving a vacancy, and Jim Lamson was President of the (Fusionist) Senate. So Jim Lamson became Maine's Governor No. 4 in the year 1880, except that General Joshua L. Chamberlain wanted to wait on the Supreme Court, and the good general refused in his pleasant way to recognize Governor Lamson. Instead, General Chamberlain felt things had simmered down and he could go home, so he asked Mayor Nash of Augusta to stand by. Mayor Nash interpreted this as an appointment to be "acting governor" without portfolio, so he put the Augusta police in charge of the cannon on the statehouse steps and became Maine's Governor No. 5 for the time being. On one occasion he called in quarry workers from Hallowell and deputized them as assistant governors.

In charge of the statehouse for the time being, Gov-

ernor Nash was conciliatory, and felt it would be all
right if the Republican House met in the evenings after
the Fusionist House had adjourned for the day. At this
point, somebody reported that the state seal had been
lost. This was a bit unhandy with two sets of legisla-
tures going at once, and Governor Nash and his stone-
quarry deputies bent every effort to find out who stole
it.

Meantime, with a place to meet, the Republican Senate now organized and elected Joseph A. Locke of Cum-
berland County as President. This placed him on equal
footing with Jim Lamson, so Joseph A. Locke became
Maine's Governor No. 6 for the year 1880. It would be
his move to become governor in fact just as soon as he
could find a vacancy. For some time now, the Fusionist
legislature met by day and enacted various laws, and
the Republican legislature would meet in the evening
and repeal them.

When the Fusionist House of Representatives bal-
loted for governor, Joseph L. Smith, who had been the
Greenback candidate, was elected. He was sworn in with
solemnity and dignity—becoming Maine's governor No.
7 for the year 1880.

Since the state seal hadn't been found, there was
enough delay in the ascension of Governor Smith VII
so the Republican House could organize by lamplight
and get down to the business of electing Daniel F. Davis
of the town of Corinth to the governorship. By this time
the Supreme Court had found in favor of the Republicans on every count, so Daniel F. Davis was inaugu-
rated Governor of Maine in fact—Maine's Governor No.
8 for the year 1880, and the true governor. It turned
out that Governor Davis knew where the state seal was
all the time, and he drew it from his pocket and certified

his authority. The members of the Supreme Court were in the receiving line. The next morning the Fusionist legislature met on the sidewalk out front of the statehouse and adjourned to reassemble at the Augusta City Hall for further business. But it never met again. Those who had really been elected joined the real legislature, and those who had spuriously been counted in went home.

The confusion throughout the state was real during all this. Lot Morrill and Bill Fessenden depended on home state support to hold their places in Washington, so they came often to make speeches at "money meetings" and try to bring sense to the Greenbackers. These money meetings were not always orderly. Then there was a codger from the Turner-Buckfield "deestrick" by the name of Solon Chase, who teamed a yoke of oxen all over the state and made Greenback speeches from the cart. His theme was that he'd spent good money for his steers, but now they weren't worth all that. True, he was confusing "hard money" with inflation, but he convinced a lot of canny Mainers—enough to bring on eight governors in one year. Solon Chase used to wave his goadstick and shout, "Lookit them steers!" For a long time "Lookit them steers!" was a Maine pleasantry to demolish anybody who said something foolish.

The militia got a good workout during all this, but open warfare never broke out. Mostly, one governor would call up the militia and another governor would order it to disperse. The nearest anything came to what might be called an incident was a small exercise at Bangor. One governor ordered the militia to move munitions to Augusta, to preserve the safety of the state, and when the wagon of powder got on the bridge over the Kenduskeag River, a bunch of Republicans stood in its way. Some Greenbackers in the background cheered and urged the wagon on, and the soldier-boy holding the reins was clearly in a perplexity. The Republicans told him if he didn't turn around and drive back to the armory they'd tip his wagon into the Kenduskeag River—horses, powder, him, and all. The driver said he'd need a few moments to consider his options, and they gave him three seconds. Showing wisdom, he turned his team and thus saved his own life. That's as close to bloodshed as the state came in this disturbing period. The cannon Governor Joshua L. Chamberlain had on the porch of the statehouse were never fired—some say they were never loaded.

Meantime the constitution had been amended to provide for biennial elections and a plurality vote. The real Governor Davis ran for reelection, but was defeated by a Fusionist candidate, General Harris M. Plaisted. This perhaps vindicated the Greenback-Democrat contentions, but at the same time the Republicans gained good majorities in both the House and Senate. Many votes in that election were cast for *Harrison* M. Plaisted instead of Harris M. Plaisted. This was most certainly an irregularity, but nobody made an issue of it—the Republicans wouldn't have touched it with a ten-foot pole.

15

How Maine boys participated in
the tragic War Between the
States, in particular the heroic
actions of Benjamin Franklin
Farrar, the butcher's son, and his
liberation of two Rebel geese at
the Battle of Gettysburgh.

Millions of man hours have been spent in research,
thousands of scholars have bent every effort, and tens
of millions of words have been written about our War
Between the States. The strategies of General Robert
E. Lee have been analyzed, the exasperations of President Abraham Lincoln itemized, the morality of General William T. Sherman investigated. But until now
nobody has told the story of the Civil War in terms of
Benjamin Franklin Farrar, who was a private in Company I of the Sixteenth Maine Regiment of Volunteers.
He found the war a frustrating interlude in his other-

wise placid life, which lasted into his eighties, when he died in bed. He had enlisted when he was twenty-two, in the year 1862.

The Sixteenth Maine was mostly recruited from the farms and small villages, which is important to his story. Benjamin Franklin Farrar was called Frank, and in Maine his last name is pronounced *farrer*, not the hoity-toity far-RAH used later by the soprano Geraldine. Geraldine Farrar and Frank Farrar were buttonhole cousins of a sort, but they never met. Frank lived at "The Factory," which was a section of Maine's town of Lisbon, and his father had a slaughterhouse and ran a meat business. Frank was, at twenty-two, fully competent in his father's footsteps, and one day would take over the business. But the year was 1862, and before Frank would become proprietor he had to fight, and win, the Civil War, free the slaves, and save the Union.

The reverses suffered by the Union army in the first year of that war had left the North looking less than heroic, and President Lincoln's call for more soldiers early in 1862 was frantic. Orders came to recruit the Sixteenth Maine Regiment of Volunteers—886 men and not more than 1,046, able-bodied and between eighteen and forty-five, to sign up for three years or the duration.

Now, the wife of a Bowdoin College professor had written *Uncle Tom's Cabin* to stir the country's emotions, but it hadn't done all that much to whip up the State-o'-Mainers. Mainers knew the war would ruin their maritime prosperity, and once a ship is tied up in port the expenses flourish. Slavery, which Maine didn't practice, wasn't accepted as a cause or a reason. The war, to Mainers, was an economic and industrial consequence of Northern development, something that left the South no solution other than a fight. *That* fight had already been won.

So when Father Abraham called for soldiers, they were hard to find. Maine didn't rally 'round to join the Sixteenth Regiment. The order to recruit the regiment came on May 1, and within that month Governor Israel Washburn (one of the remarkable Washburn boys) realized his people needed a pep talk. He issued a flag-waving proclamation to answer the state's disinclination to be patriotic. He said we must not falter or fail. He urged that everybody join in to bring this war to a speedy and glorious issue. He wanted the light of Maine's shining example to brighten and guide, to cheer and to bless the nation. Peace and tranquillity must be restored and our principles must be preserved. He played *Vox Humana*.

Maine's adjutant general at that time was John L. Hodson, and he picked up the refrain with a proclamation that began, "Citizen Soldiers!" There was a country to be saved, and he said, "You are the only ones who can render most efficient aid in this holy and patriotic work." The newspapers of Maine then joined in this Wimpyism of "let's you and him fight!" and editors deplored the state's reluctance to rally to this great cause. Posters appeared on barns and fence posts, and the ministers preached patriotism from the pulpits. This bombardment of encouragement did penetrate the state's lethargy, and by August 960 men, mostly eighteen-year-olds, had signed up. Frank Farrar, too.

None of the enlisted men had seen any military service; not many had ever been away from home before. None of the line officers had military experience. One staff officer seemed a likely choice; an editorial said "His long and successful business life eminently fits him for the position." Without the slightest training, the regiment was put on a train for Boston and left Augusta on August 14, the day after "mustering in." At Boston the men had sandwiches, entrained again for Fall River, and aboard the steamer *Commonwealth* went by night to Jersey City. For the next several days the regiment marched to Philadelphia, to Baltimore, and to Washington. On August 21 the Sixteenth Maine left Washington, crossing the Long Bridge, and marched six miles to Camp Casey, to bivouac that night "on the dirtiest soil that could be found in the dirty state of Virginia." The Sixteenth Maine rested there for two days, then resumed march to Camp Whipple, near Fort Tillinghast, and joined the First Brigade, ready to be sent into battle. As the boys from Maine were making camp, they looked up to see the Massachusetts Fourteenth pass in quick time to take part in the battles at Bull Run. And before the boys from Maine were settled in, they looked up again to see the same Massachusetts Fourteenth coming back—beaten, bloody, weary, without equipment. Nobody ever left Maine and went so far in such a short time!

That night the Maine boys tried to get some sleep, but cannon at a distance didn't help, and at two o'clock in the morning came the long roll for everybody to turn out and form line of battle. The commanding general, if any, hadn't confided, so nobody knew what this was all about, but the regiment held position until sunrise. Nothing had happened. And for Frank Farrar and his comrades, nothing was going to happen for quite some time. The First Brigade was to move on to Fredericksburgh, and the Sixteen Maine with it, but the War Department managed to forget all about the Sixteenth Maine, and for the next few weeks no supplies were received. Not only that, but haversacks, tents, personal things, all but muskets and ammunition, were stored in Washington so the regiment could "travel light."

Thus began the hardships of the "Blanket Brigade." This name was applied because in a short time the men were destitute of clothing, and for warmth and modesty wrapped themselves in their blankets. Lieutenant Colonel Charles W. Tilden, commanding the Sixteenth Maine, began his fruitless effort to get supplies and to have the regiment's stores brought forward from Washington. His series of letters tells the whole story of Benjamin Franklin Farrar's experiences in the Civil War. Appeals for food and clothing were returned, marked "Disapproved." On bivouac, the men made shelters from cornstocks. And for food . . .

For food, Frank Farrar went on a skirmish. The dictionary defines "skirmish," but not the kind Frank Farrar organized. On his first skirmish Frank and friends went ahead of the Union advance posts, into Rebel territory, and "captured a black pig, seven hens, and considerable leaf tobacco." It was nothing for Frank Farrar to butcher a hog, and from then on the Sixteenth Maine didn't wait on wagons of food from the rear. When at last supplies began to arrive and the urgency was over, these skirmishes continued. On one occasion Frank was returning with his platoon and came upon a staff officer and his aides, all mounted, and there might have been some questions. The boys had bags of hens, a beef calf on a carrying pole, and a washtub of excellent honey. But the officer, well knowing how the War Department had abused the Sixteenth Maine, quickly ordered eyes right, and Frank's platoon passed without breaking step. That night the staff officer was glad for what he had done—he found a cut of honey by his bed. The officer said later that the Sixteenth Maine were poor soldiers but the finest scavengers in the Union army.

Colonel Tilden was still trying to get messages to the right officers, to have things brought forward from storage, and was still getting "disapproved," when orders came to reduce the Sixteenth Maine to battle gear and proceed. This meant two days' rations and forty rounds of musket ammunition, plus a fifteen-mile march on the way to Ridgeville and to Fredericksburgh. That night the men ate their two days' rations, and still no wagons came. Sickness set in. Men dropped from the march and were sent back to a Washington hospital. Some men died in camp. The foragers were unable to skirmish enough food. Colonel Tilden wrote, "Many of my men have no shoes to their feet or shirts to their backs, and none has had a change of underwear since Fort Tillinghast." None had an overcoat, none had shelter-tent.

When at last Colonel Tilden got "approved," a quartermaster refused to move things, and when he did move them they got sent to Sharpsburgh instead of Hagerstown. On November 13, 1862, a medical director inspected the Sixteenth Maine and found the strength to be 693 men, of whom 181 were under treatment by the regimental surgeon. He ascribed the illnesses to lack of clothing, and said 34 men had no clothing at all. And the "Blanket Brigade" was on its way to Fredericksburgh, where the battle began on December 13.

Colonel Tilden, commanding the Sixteenth Maine, made contact with the Rebels, but his fire had no effect on them because of the breastworks thrown up. Accordingly, Colonel Tilden asked for and received (from Colonel Adrien Root, commanding the First Brigade) permission to fix bayonets and charge. Thus the Sixteenth Maine, and Frank Farrar, went into their first battle, driving the Rebels from their breastworks. Twenty-two Maine boys fell in that action. But weary, hungry, cold, heartsick, and ridiculed, they fixed bayonets and charged, and there they were in the advance of the Union attack, hanging on until everybody else should catch up. Then Colonel Tilden saw that nobody was trying to catch up, and here he was, with his men, exposed and vulnerable. Lacking support, he called for withdrawal, and the Sixteenth Maine retired. Somehow, and he would never tell how, Frank Farrar brought a yearling bull back from the fray, and after he conducted a proper funeral for the beast the Sixteenth Maine feasted before dropping to the ground for a night's sleep.

Then the war ran along, and the Sixteenth Maine came to Gettysburgh. Still miserably clothed and poorly fed, except by its foragers, the regiment now counted 267 men and 25 officers. It was thrown into combat at Little Round Top on the first day of that battle, and Colonel Tilden had orders to hold his position at all costs. The regimental historian wrote later, "The 16th Maine was the last regiment that left the extreme front, July 1st— if four officers and 38 men can be called a regiment." Benjamin Franklin Farrar did not return that evening with his Company I, and as he was not found among the slain, the company clerk marked him "deserted."

But Benjamin Franklin Farrar crept into camp after dark that night; he hadn't deserted at all. He had, rather, been captured, and as a prisoner had been sent behind the lines. Because of certain confusion that prevailed, there was some laxity about his being guarded—after all, there *was* a battle going on—so Frank had looked around and had found a pair of geese that took his fancy. He did them in, and then worked his way back to the

Union lines and joined his friends. He had a great welt of a bruise on his right shoulder where a Rebel had hit him with the but of a musket and knocked him down. It hurt some sore, and Frank hadn't enjoyed crawling back and dragging those two honkers by their necks.

Fifty years later—that would be in 1913—Uncle Sam threw a big reunion party for the surviving Union veterans of the Battle of Gettysburgh. Word came that railroad tickets would be provided and expenses paid, and every GAR hall in the country was agog. The veterans would assemble on the old battlefield, now a national shrine. The Women's Relief Corps put on bake sales to raise pocket money for the veterans, and so did the "tents" of the Sons and Daughters of Union Veterans. Frank Farrar and all the others of the Sixteenth Maine Regiment of Volunteers made preparations for the trip. But when the invitations and the railway passes came in the mail Frank Farrar didn't get his. Dan Small got his, and so did Ephraim Jordan. And the Cotton brothers. But not Benjamin Franklin Farrar.

Some mistake somewhere, so inquiry was made with the adjutant general at the statehouse in Augusta, and he said he'd look into the matter. But nobody heard anything from him, and time was running along. Dan Small took it upon himself to go to Augusta and get an answer, and the adjutant general told him Benjamin Franklin Farrar was not entitled to go—that the records show he deserted at Gettysburgh. It just goes to show what records amount to. Frank had been getting his pension all those years, and he had been given his soldier's bonus, all right.

By this time all the veterans (they were called comrades) agreed they wouldn't go if Frank didn't go, and there was even talk of passing the hat to pay Frank's way if he didn't get his invitation and tickets in time. But when Dan Small came back with the news that Frank Farrar had deserted, all his comrades hurried to a justice of the peace and made affidavit that the War Department had made *another* mistake. That was the way they worded things—the Sixteenth Maine Regiment had lived through the bumblings, boobishness, errors, mistakes, goofs, and sundry idiocies of the "Blanket Brigade," and now this was just *another*. Frank went to Gettysburgh with his comrades, but things at the battlefield had changed so that he couldn't quite find the place where he got the two geese.

16

**How a Maine man dreamed of a
great railroad system that would
bring all of Canada and all of the
Golden West to the seaports of
Maine; the Furbishes, the
lousewort, and the demise of the
Great North American &
European Railroad.**

On a typical Maine June morning in the year 1935, a
heavily clothed gentleman, wearing mittens and earmuffs and jauntily sporting an ebony walking stick,
paused at 75 Maine Street in Brunswick, looked up and
down, and stepped inside. The pleasant warmth of the
interior felt good to him after the bracing outside air of
the lingering Maine summer, and he brushed the icicles
from his bushy eyebrows, removed his mittens, and
opened his briefcase. The aroma of printer's ink was
heavy, because 75 Maine Street was a printing plant,

and from the doorway leading to the "chapel" he could hear the unrelenting repetition of a Chandler & Price, with the friendly jingling of the ratchets on the inking plate as the rollers participated in their intended purposes.

"Good morning, Mr. Furbish," said the young lady at the counter (for the man was, indeed, Mr. Furbish), "isn't it good to have some warmer weather for a change?"

Removing his hat (as a gentleman should, and Mr. Furbish always did) and pushing his earmuffs forward over his temples, Mr. Furbish said, "Good morning, Miss Knox! Yes, it certainly is—if this keeps up we can take off the storm windows!" He handed her several sheets of paper he had taken from his briefcase.

"My, my," said Miss Knox, "is it letterhead time again?"

"Yes. May I have the usual?"

"Certainly. Let me see—a thousand letterheads, a thousand bill heads, and a thousand number six envelopes."

"That is correct, and shall I come in on Friday afternoon?"

"Friday is fine, Mr. Furbish."

"Thank you," and Mr. Furbish adjusted his earmuffs, replaced his hat, drew his overcoat collar about his neck, ran his hands into his mittens, held his walking stick and his briefcase in his left hand while he opened the door with his right, and he stepped out to the street to continue on his way to the post office. He paused to speak to people he met, lifting his hat to the ladies, and that was the last transaction on record which involved the Great North American & European Railroad. Mr. Furbish died in 1936 at the age of sixty-two, well before he had used his last order of railroad stationery. Mr.

Furbish had been born in Brunswick of a venerable
Brunswick family, the son of John and Maria Day Furbish. Nobody now knows how he came to own the Great
North American & European Railroad, but its corporate existence ended with Mr. Samuel Furbish.

His brother was Benjamin Furbish, who kept the
hardware store under the name of Eaton Hardware—
later to be sold to Jim Black and to become Black's
Hardware. Benjamin was known far and wide for his
meticulous work in varnishing buggies. To have your
buggy varnished by Ben Furbish was to be in the Cad-
illac and Rolls-Royce set, or at least in the Baldwin and
Mason & Hamlin set, and one of his "jobs" could be
identified far down the street. Ben built up coats after
coats of varnish until a buggy had the glassy finish of a
grand piano. He did this work on the upper floor of his
store, in a room specially designed to deter dust. He
had a tentlike hood that lifted and lowered by ropes
through pulleys, and when a coat of varnish had been
applied, he would lower this tent over the buggy to further fend off dust. Ben's usual treatment called for eight
coats of varnish, of which the first seven were patiently
rubbed down with pumice stone and oil to "cuff off the
gloss" before the next coat was added. Sixteen days were
allowed for drying between coats. The eighth coat would
shine like a star.

When Jim Black acquired the old Eaton store after
Benjamin died, the inventory of stock showed things
like horseshoe nails, drip pans for ice chests, butter
molds, and many other items left over from a forgotten
past, which Jim marked up 300 percent and sold as
authentic antiques. Benjamin Furbish kept that kind of
a store; a good store.

Samuel and Benjamin Furbish were cousins to Kate

Furbish, the botanist. Miss Furbish, as a lady scientist of note, deserves everybody's special thanks for saving Maine's St. John River from the philanderings of the Army Corps of Engineers and others bent on damming it to the extinction of its natural condition. As a belated afterthought of the Passamaquoddy Bay Tidal Project, the big boondoggle of Franklin Delano Roosevelt's New Deal, several alternative proposals for hydroelectric power had their day, and it was hard to convince the boondogglers and get them off our backs. For a time it looked as if a dam was going to prevail on the upper St. John River—one of the world's loveliest rivers—and contribute Maine's wilderness beauty to the heating of curling irons in New Jersey, a generosity no Mainer cheered about. Cousin Kate Furbish was by now long gone, but in her active days she had roamed the Maine woods and set down all manner of information about the flowers and shrubs and ferns. The St. John River valley, she wrote, is the last place to find Furbish's lousewort. Kate Furbish gave the plant her name.

The lousewort really isn't very much. The Latin, or scientific, name is *Pedicularis*, from *pediculus*, a louse. 'Tis said that farmers used to believe the plant nurtured a certain louse, or insect, that was responsible for a skin disease amongst sheep. Maybe so, but one lousewort became Furbish's lousewort and reposed in lonely fashion along the St. John River. It had been on the list of endangered species for many years before the dam on that river was proposed, and lo! there was now ample legislation forbidding abuse to endangered species! Thanks to Furbish's lousewort, the St. John River flows as before.

Kate's cousin Sam was also a scholar, and a gentleman as well. He carried himself always in the devout posture of a clergyman arriving for his pulpit test. He never dangled a participle or split an infinitive, and he never hemmed or went "er" and "ah" when he spoke. For many years he was Grand Lecturer of the Grand Masonic Lodge of Maine, and as a student of Masonic affairs had acquired infinite knowledge in related subjects such as grammar, rhetoric, logic, arithmetic, geometry, music, and astronomy. As Grand Lecturer he was responsible for the purity of the ritual, and he visited about the state to instruct the officers of subordinate lodges. His posture and appearance are thus explained; he comported himself with the dignity and assurance that went with his knowledge and circumspection. Nobody can tell how Samuel Furbish came to acquire the controlling interest in the great North American & European Railroad, but he had served as treasurer of Bowdoin College for twenty-three years and may have gained insight into financial affairs in that way. Everybody else had forgotten all about the Great North American & European Railroad long years ago.

The history of Maine railroading would drive a serious historian plain nuts in no time—although that would perhaps be a putt rather than a drive. The general topic began with simple decisions here and there to the effect of "Hey! Let's build a railroad!" All of Maine's railroads began with a small plan for a small area, and a big debt. Seafaring was in the Maine bloodstream to the extent that every proposed line was meant to be a feeder to the saltwater harbors—a facility to bring cargo from inland to Maine ships waiting at Maine wharves. The first railroad in Maine had "rails" made of strap iron fastened to wooden timbers, and horses pulled the small cars from

Woodland down to the Calais waterfront. After that, other railroads would do the same for Portland, Wiscasset, Bath, Rockland, Bangor and Brewer, and Belfast.

The financial finagling that went on over finding the money to build railroads went about the same each time a new short line was proposed. The Maine legislature passed an act making it lawful for towns and cities to buy railroad bonds and stocks, and as such towns presumed the railroads would boost prosperity, it wasn't hard for the promoters to get local appropriations. Then the legislature would grant public lands—of which the state then had many—so that each incorporation of a railroad company would be followed by a big land sale. The pattern seemed to be that as soon as a railroad was completed, or even partly constructed, the company would go bankrupt, default on its obligations, and while the directors met each morning at the bank, the creditors had the satisfaction of bringing prosperity to their communities. At about the time the Calais railroad was going into bankruptcy for the first time, there began to appear the nest-egg idea of the Maine Central Railroad system, one day to be the state's principal system, and one by one the little railroads would be leased to the Maine Central for 999 years. (It would be a short 999—the MCRR sold out in 1987.)

But before the Maine Central system took shape, there appeared one John Alfred Poor, who in 1836 was a practicing lawyer in Bangor. He was born in Andover, over towards the White Mountains of New Hampshire, so he well knew the inland importance of access to the sea. He was first interested in the Bangor Piscataquis Canal & Railroad Company, which had lately taken over the franchise of the bankrupt Old Town Railroad. By either name, this was a timber and strap iron line with the typical purpose of bringing freight to the water-front. Poor watched this refinancing take over, but he saw farther than anybody else at the moment. He even envisioned more than the yet-to-be Maine Central System. Why not, he reasoned, one great railroad that would not only serve the state, but would link the Maine harbors to all of Canada and our own western lands?

In those days a railroad over the mountains into Vermont was still far ahead of its time, and Poor already saw that as just a part of his scheme to bring Montreal down to Portland vessels. Then there was the big hump of Maine's Aroostook County blocking Canada's route to her own Atlantic ports. Poor thus foresaw both the Grand Trunk line down to Portland and the Canadian Pacific route linking the Great Lakes and the St. Lawrence River to St. John and Halifax. Understand, Poor was never a railroad operator—he projected plans, selected routes, worked out finances, and went after franchises as needed. His activities took the form of a dreamboat corporation named the Great North American & European Railroad Company. It would be great fun to say this railroad never existed, just for the sake of a better yarn, but it did.

Boston interests had already built tracks to Portsmouth, New Hampshire, and shortly these would be extended to Portland in Maine. Poor, as a Mainer, felt we should keep our business for our own ships and our own ports. Canada, at that time without railroads, embraced Poor's proposals and never gave great thought to Boston. The St. Lawrence River froze every winter, so lines from Montreal to both Portland and to Halifax and St. John made sense. Poor didn't live to see his big dream of an integrated railroad system serving Maine come to pass, but he saw a good deal of it take shape, and he believed ardently in the need for it. He foresaw what is still the Bangor & Aroostook, and he played a part in getting New Brunswick tracks over to Fort Fairfield, Houlton, and Presque Isle. His big idea, and the one that gave the name to his holding company, was the line from Lac Mégantic, Québec, through the Maine wilderness to McAdam Junction, New Brunswick.

So in time all the little railroads of Maine fitted into the pattern that prevailed into the 1930s, when the railroads fell upon evil days. Except that here and there the Great North American & European Railroad Company retained odd and unrelated interests. Here and there a bond outstanding. Maybe rental on a sidetrack. Perhaps royalty due on a franchise. Trackage—that good money one railroad pays to another for use of the line. Whatever remained, Sammie Furbish picked it up, and every so often he needed some stationery. The Great North American & European always sent out its bills on time. It brought Sammie sufficient income for living well, and allowed him ample time for his Masonic studies. Just before his death in 1936 his Masonic faithfulness brought him the honor of being named Deputy Grand Master.

17

The story of an out-of-state
hunter who got lost in the Maine
woods and thus gained great
fame; the same also being a
valuable lesson in the art of
editing a newspaper so the
circulation grows.

Every thorough study of Maine affairs will have at least
one manhunt—the lost hunter in the Maine woods comes
and goes, a dime a dozen. The greatest manhunt in the
history of the Maine woods took place in 1930, its sce-
nario typical of many another. The success of any search
for a lost hunter depends on the Boston newspapers,
and in 1930 the sponsor of the Kaufman search was the
Boston *Post*. The idea was to get the most out of it, and
in 1930 the *Post* had the largest morning circulation of
any standard United States newspaper and its circula-

tion in Maine was greater than the combined circulation of all other newspapers circulating in the state.

Mitchell B. Kaufman, president of Boston's Converse Rubber Company, had gone with some friends on a hunting trip to northern Somerset County—the party stayed at the Crocker Pond Camps in the wild land township of Dennistown, not far from the Maine-Québec boundary. The nearest community of size was Jackman. In those days the *Post* received its back-country news from correspondents who were called "stringers." The stringer for Somerset County was Roland T. Patten, then editor of the Skowhegan *Independent-Reporter*. Whenever Patten had something he thought the *Post* would use, he would "query" by telegraph. So on the eighth of November, 1930, Mr. Patten learned from his own correspondent in Jackman that a hunter had been lost, and he queried the *Post*.

Let us not forget that a few years before that, the *Post* had fomented, thought up, invented, fabricated, and otherwise brought about the amazing tale of Joe Knowles and how he survived in the Maine woods the way Tarzan of the Apes had survived in Africa. Joe Knowles became an international sensation, owned lock, stock, and barrel by the Boston *Post*, and anything out of the Maine woods was a natural. The city editor of the *Post* was Edward J. Dunn, truly the last of the great American city editors. Eddie never missed an opportunity. A hunter lost was a headline gained, and Eddie wired back to Roland Patten, "Send 500 words."

Patten's story in the *Post* on the morning of November 9 received front-page space. The headlines ran: "MAN LOST IN FOREST—PRESIDENT OF CONVERSE RUBBER COMPANY SOUGHT IN VAIN FOR FOUR DAYS —SEPARATED FROM GUIDE IN MAINE WOODS—MITCHELL B. KAUFMAN, 37 YEARS,

FROM BOSTON—WHILE STAYING AT THE CROCKER POND CAMPS." But a stringer like Roland T. Patten didn't always get to follow up his own story in the *Post*. Now Eddie Dunn looked over his stable and he picked out Elliot Norton. Elliot Norton was to become New England's foremost drama critic, but in 1930 he was a "cub" on the *Post* staff and had yet to work on a "big" story. Dunn was criticized for selecting an inexperienced reporter for a Maine woods job, but Eddie was a judge of talent and he saw Norton as a comer. So Elliot Norton took the next train out of North Station and was on his way. It was a long ride to Jackman—to Portland, to Bangor, to Mattawamkeag, and then by Canadian Pacific to Jackman.

Norton introduced himself where it mattered, and picked up where Roland T. Patten had left off. Norton's successive stories on the front page of the *Post* proved immediately that Dunn had made no mistake in picking him. There are certain things reporters must say, and Norton knew what they were and when to say them. First, he asked the sheriff, "Are you planning to use bloodhounds?" The answer to this is "We have not yet ruled out the possibility." Similarly, with a fire you ask if arson is suspected, and with a death you ask if there is foul play. The sheriff had to tell Norton that he was sorry, but Somerset County didn't have any bloodhounds.

This might well be a police problem, but it was not a journalistic problem. Back in Boston Eddie Dunn had a little difficulty finding any bloodhounds, but he came up with a pack, and then he found somebody to crate them. They had to come to Jackman by railway express via Montreal, but they covered the exclusive *Post* headline: "BLOODHOUNDS BROUGHT IN FOR KAUFMAN SEARCH."

Norton's story of November 12 contained an error. He said searchers had found a "shack" near the Canadian line where Kaufman might have taken shelter while wandering. The next morning everybody in Jackman read the *Post* and told Norton a shack in the Maine woods is a "camp."

The daily story on the front page of the *Post* caused other newspapers to give heed to the Kaufman search; by now Jackman was full of "trained seals," and the pressure on the sheriff and his searchers was terrific. But Norton had ingratiated himself, and Sheriff Markham favored the *Post* when he passed out news. Now the search was winding down and in a few days would be called off: "SEARCH OF KAUFMAN NEARS CLOSE—SNOW NOW FALLING MAY PUT END TO WORK." So Norton asked, "Do you suspect foul play?" Until this time nobody had said anything about foul play, so this opened a whole new line of thought: "NOW THINK KAUFMAN IS GUN VICTIM." On November 19: "FOUL PLAY THEORY IS ACCEPTED—SHERIFF WILL REOPEN PROBE OF KAUFMAN CASE." On November 23: "DIVERS SEARCH POND BOTTOM WITH NO RESULT." On November 24: "KAUFMAUN'S BODY NOT IN MAINE POND."

By now a thousand searchers had covered six hundred square miles of northern Somerset County, and Norton reported that the search was costing $5,000 a day. A friend offered a $10,000 reward to anybody who found Kaufman—dead or living. Things were tapering off, but Norton was not discouraged: "ARREST IN KAUFMAN CASE NEAR—CARTRIDGE CASE FOUND WHICH IS EXPECTED TO SOLVE MYSTERY—NEW DEVELOPMENTS—GREAT SECRECY KEPT—FEEL CERTAIN MAN WAS SLAIN."

By this time everybody was telling Norton that Kaufman had wandered off and died in the woods, but a good reporter wouldn't be led astray by *that!* However, Norton did have to report: "FIFTY MEN STAY ON KAUFMAN HUNT," and as things began to lag the *Post* (or Eddie Dunn) managed to start a rumor that Kaufman had been seen in a Boston Hotel: "POLICE COMB BACK BAY DISTRICT." For a few days the story hovered between Boston and Jackman, but Kaufman wasn't found on either end. On December 11 Kaufman's estate was listed for probation: "ESTIMATED $375,000."

On the strength of this the *Post* began referring to Kaufman as "missing tycoon." Meantime, back in Jackman, Norton found a flashlight in the woods and offered it as a "clue," but one of the guides said it was his. As a parting shot, Norton offered an accident: "KAUFMAN NEAR FRIEND'S PATH—SHERIFF LEARNS MISSING TYCOON WALKED INTO DIRECT LINE OF FIRE AND MIGHT POSSIBLY HAVE BEEN UNKNOWINGLY SHOT—GUIDES ELIMINATED FROM CONNECTION—MYSTERY GROWS DEEPER—CARD GAME MAY BE CLUE."

But winter was drawing on and snow had covered the Great North Countree. Norton and Dunn might have thought up numerous new angles, but without the sheriff's men in the woods it was hard to continue the hunt. Elliot Norton shook hands with all the good friends he had made in the Jackman area, and returned to Boston to put in a dreary winter with routine stories about subway tie-ups, fires in the North End, and lost children at the Joy Street Station. But he did keep in touch with Jackman, and his headline of December 14 was not to be the end of his story: "KAUFMAN HUNT LEAVES WOODS."

It was in April that he called Sheriff Markham on the telephone and was able to resume: "RESUME HUNT FOR BODY OF HUB MAGNATE." On April 28, 1931: "KAUFMAN SEARCH IS ON AGAIN—SNOW STILL TWO FEET DEEP HERE."

Elliot Norton didn't return to Jackman. He didn't have to. He had made a friend of Sheriff Markham, and Sheriff Markham told him all he needed to know over the telephone. On May 18: "SHERIFF TO TALK AGAIN WITH GUIDE—LAST TO SEE KAUFMAN ALIVE IN MAINE WOODS." By this time all the other newspapers were trying to catch up to Elliot Norton, and just about everything he reported today was in the other papers tomorrow. And it was on the morning of May 18, 1936, that the *Post* front page was almost given over entirely to these headlines: "KAUFMAN'S BODY FOUND NEAR CANADA—THE BOSTON POST IN A COPYRIGHTED ARTICLE SAYS THAT THE BODY OF MITCHELL B. KAUFMAN, MISSING PRESIDENT OF THE CONVERSE RUBBER COMPANY, WAS FOUND TODAY NEAR ST. THEOPHILE, QUEBEC."

Within minutes of the finding of the body, Sheriff Markham was on the telephone, and Elliot Norton had an "exclusive." The "find" was not made public until the *Post* had papers on the street. Norton's copyrighted story said that three Maine guides from Jackman had found the body—Lawrence Hughey, Harry Hughey, and Farnsworth J. "Teddy" Wilson. They would share the reward. Kaufman had died of exposure. There was no evidence of "foul play." Identification was positive. During the next few days Elliot Norton brought his manhunt to an end with several unsensational addenda. The Kaufman will was probated, previous to which his body was brought from Jackman to West Roxbury for burial. It was now May 24.

On June 23 the *Post* ran Norton's final copy on the biggest manhunt in the history of the Maine woods. He said the search had cost $40,000 (he didn't include what Eddie Dunn had paid to rent bloodhounds). He said James H. Murtha of Jackman had filed suit against the

Kaufman estate for non-payment of wages. Murtha had directed the search and didn't get paid.

And wouldn't you know—there are still people in the Jackman region who will tell you the body found was not that of Mitchell B. Kaufman, the late resident of Massachusetts. They don't say who it was instead, but whoever it was is buried in West Roxbury.

18

About William King, who had a
yoke of black steers and guided
them as the crow flies to fame
and prosperity. He was governor
of Maine, but was never president
of the United States or sold
automobiles.

Every February the automobile dealers of the State of
Maine join in the annual "Presidents' Sale," and by the
first of March everybody owns a new car and quite a
few people leave for Florida. It is an extremely emo-
tional experience to see General George Washington
enduring the rigors of Valley Forge, leading a white
horse through the deep snow, his tricorn hat braving
the frigid blast, and hear him recite the credit terms on
a new Chevrolet. Patriotism bubbles over as we watch
Honest Abraham Lincoln put a match to a Paul Revere
lantern (the one if by land) and take us into a warehouse

of GMC trucks. Abraham Lincoln says, "Four score and seventeen dollars ago, my father would have bought a yoke of oxen . . ." Then comes March, and the Ides of March is State of Maine Day. Maine was admitted to the Union, the twenty-third state, on March 15, 1820, and her first (and best) governor was William King— who never ran for the presidency and can never take part in the "Presidents' Sale."

The nearest Maine ever came to the presidency was Hannibal Hamlin. Hamlin was born at Paris Hill in 1809, and was Maine's first Republican governor, an honor that accrued to him as one of the founders of the Republican party. He served as vice president during Lincoln's first term, but because of political bedfellowing brought on by the Civil War, Lincoln ditched Hamlin and took on Andrew Johnson (born in North Carolina). Thus Johnson, and not Hamlin, assumed the presidency when Lincoln was assassinated. Other than that, Maine has had but near misses. Senator Margaret Chase Smith was nominated for the presidency at the Republican Convention of 1964. A native of Skowhegan, she had served in Congress and was the first woman to serve in the Senate. The nomination was purely honorary, and Mrs. Smith declined graciously on the grounds that it was not her turn. James G. Blaine (from away, but then a resident of Augusta) was the Republican nominee in 1884, but was nudged by Democrat Grover Cleveland (born in New Jersey) because of the dirty pool of "Rum, Romanism, and Rebellion." Blaine had been just about everything else in Washington, and was expected to win. He had a fine reputation as "the continental liar from the State of Maine."

Then there was Nelson Rockefeller, born at Bar Harbor but really a summercater, who was vice president

under Gerald Ford. Some of his friends expected
Edmund S. Muskie, born in Rumford, to do better—
he was a vice-presidential candidate in 1968, and made
a small sally for the presidency in 1972. He did serve a
short time as secretary of state. So did Elihu Washburn,
one of the seven remarkable Washburn boys of Liver-
more. All became successful and famous, and Elihu
might well have gone on to the presidency after being
secretary of state. But he added an *e* to his family name
and became Elihu Washburne, and nobody knew who
he was.

Maine had from time to time other good men in
Washington who might have become president: Thomas
B. Reed, Lot Morrill, Bill Fessenden, Bill Frye, maybe
one of the Hales, and perhaps some others.

But William King made only one appearance on the
national scene and otherwise stuck to his affairs at home.
He was born at Scarborough and his father died when
Bill was a boy—willing him a yoke of black steers. He
set out with his young oxen to make his fortune, and
came to the fork in the road where one might haw to
Boston or gee back into the wilderness of Maine. Pondering, the lad stood there to let his cattle graze a bit,
and as he did a crow flew over. Surprised to find the
boy and the steers there, the crow let out a squawk,
lifted higher, and took off. Bill decided this was a propitious omen and he turned to follow the crow, coming
finally to Bath, where he made his fortune and his
home—turning his single asset of the steers into prosperity.

William King was an advocate of separating Maine
from Massachusetts and creating a new state, but the
way this came about was not altogether a whopping vic-
tory for him. The idea of separation had a desultory

enthusiasm in Maine, and on the first vote the necessary
majority was lacking. Meantime, Maine came to have
221 organized towns by 1816, and this alarmed the sedate
Beacon Hill members of the General Court. You couldn't
turn around without bumping into some joker from
Down East, and if things kept on the way they were
going, the Commonwealth of Massachusetts would be
run by the Mainers. There was, really, something of an
idea of "good riddance" in the Bay State. But Mainers
weren't yet sold on the idea; on the second vote 17,091
ballots were cast, but 7,132 of them were negative. This
was enough to call for a constitution, however, and Bill
King was a guiding light at the convention.

By the time a ratification vote was held, Mainers were
reconciled to being on their own, and King was happy
to have his constitution in force and to be pretty much
the unanimous first governor. But then President James
Monroe (born in Virginia) recognized King's talents and
asked him to be on the commission to negotiate the ces-
sion of Florida to the United States. For a time King
left Maine, after serving one year as governor, and when
he returned home he was out of the political swim. But
he was prosperous always, a man of intense good humor
and hearty ways, and there is the reasonable presumption that if another crow had flown up and squawked,
King might have made the United States a fine president.

When he acquired timberlands in the Carrabasset
Valley, the town of Kingfield became a memorial to him,
and there are others in his hometown of Bath. His affa-
bility and his good humor would certainly have suggested charisma to the national electorate, but he might
have had a bit of trouble over his church affiliation. As
one of the elite of Bath he attended the Old North

Church, and when he brought his bride up from Boston he did cause something of a disturbance during Sunday services. She was Anne Frazier, a humdinger of the finest kind, properest of the proper, and pretty as a pail of new milk. Bath was agog at the idea of meeting this charmer, and Bill King decided to make a grand entrance.

Sunday morning he delayed until just before the offertory, and then he entered with his bride. They swept down the aisle to the King pew, and he lovingly disposed her, neatly handing her an open hymnal before he took his place beside her. The poor parson played his second fiddle softly the rest of the time; nobody's eyes were on him. Some said, after thinking things over, that Mr. King had deliberately staged a disturbance during divine worship.

Governor King was a hearty believer in a game of cards, and his card parties at his mansion in Bath were pleasant. The men played in the card room while the ladies had tea and sherry in another room, and then all joined for social purposes. The Governor was jubilant about slapping down a trump, and his jolly approval when he took a trick could be heard all over Bath. One day a sedate member of the Old North Church tried to reason with King that his devotion to cards was not morally acceptable; he told King playing cards was the same as cheating. King answered that this was precisely why he never invited him to his card parties, and more of the same, and card playing became a spiritual issue until King withdrew from the Old North Church and affiliated with the Old South Church, which was on the other end of town but not considered so snazzy. The Old South Church was liberal about playing cards, but the Old North Church came to revise its attitude a few years later, and King returned to it affably enough. He played a good hand well.

But all his days, from the time he was on his own with his inherited steers, Governor King was successful in all he undertook, and he was perfectly capable of handling the presidency of the United States with equal results. It is the nation's loss that he preferred to remain in his beloved State of Maine rather than assume the awesome responsibilities of Chief Executive. He would have made the best automobile salesmen of them all.

19

**How the famous year of the
two winters sent so many
nonseparatists to Ohio that Maine
became a state and tourists began
coming up from Massachusetts.
The summer of our discontent.
Snow in June.**

The Paul Bunyan yarn about the "year of the two winters" was not at all a tall tale—the year was 1816. That
was the year it began to "freeze for winter before it
stopped thawing in the spring," and it was the year that
decided the big issue if Maine should separate from
Massachusetts. In 1816 most of the upland villages of
Maine were newly settled, were even *being* settled, and
the pioneers had already been plagued by several summers of discontent. Corn, the essential crop of the day,
likes hot weather. Weather pleasantly described by the
old-timers as "bare-arse," meaning one could sleep

without nightshirt and sheets. On such a night the Mainer could lie abed and "hear" the corn grow. But for several summers the nights had stayed too cool for corn crops, and there was good wonder if Maine's climate could sustain the folks who had moved in. The summer of 1816 was not only cold in Maine, but spread itself over all of North America and even to Europe. Things went crazy.

January and February were mild, so overnight fires weren't necessary. Everybody thought this was a good sign and promised the summer would show some good corn weather again. But March was cold, and seemed even more so after the moderate temperatures of January and February. April grew colder as May approached. In May fruit buds were frozen, and ice stayed on the ponds into June. Gardens didn't get planted, and seeds that did sprout had their tops frozen back. Not a blade of corn showed in all of Maine, and June had a snowfall of up to a foot. There wasn't a warm day in the whole month of June, when come perfect days, and constant chill winds out of the north were dry. Woodpiles were long spent, and green wood fresh from the forest burned on every hearth. Men who tried to work out their taxes on the roads between planting and haying did what work they could in mittens and overcoats, but the ground hadn't thawed and little work got done. There was one farmer with a flock of sheep in his hillside pasture, and when it snowed he went to see if they were all right. He got lost in the snowstorm. Three days later his neighbors found him, and he had frozen his feet.

July kept right on with frost, ice, and snow. August wasn't any better, but September did warm up and offer two weeks of fairly warm days. October, however, brought back the midsummer conditions, and there was good sledding snow all through November. And—you might guess—December was mild and pleasant, too late to do any good.

So that was the year of no summer; the year of two winters. And 1816 was of the time that Maine people were considering the wisdom of separating from Massachusetts and forming their own state. One vote had already been held, but the outcome lacked the required ayes. Maine people had decided they would stay with Massachusetts. But now the bleak summer of 1816 caused a good many Maine settlers to come down with an ailment called "Ohio fever." Discouraged, they sought new homes in prairie country, and some fifteen thousand people from Maine packed up and headed west. Seemingly, the people who left Maine and went to Ohio were mostly those who had wanted to stay attached to Massachusetts. The next year another vote was taken on the separation question, and this time the ayes prevailed. Maine achieved separate statehood in 1820—on the Ides of March—and the summers have been pretty good ever since. Good enough so a lot of Massachusetts people come up here to enjoy them, and in that way we get back more than our fifteen thousand.

20

A faithful explanation of how President George Washington, when our Republic was young and untried, used his influence to aid Maine's Captain Walter Prout in his business transactions and make him a philanthropist.

When you stop to think about it, Pierre Dominique Toussaint L'Ouverture was something of a name to saddle on a black slave boy who was to die in prison. But between the cradle and the grave the fellow cut quite a caper, and for one pleasant moment he figured in State o' Maine seafaring history. It was in 1793, when the United States was a struggling new nation, that little Pierre was freed, along with all the other slaves on the Island of Hispaniola, by its French owners. He became a great advocate of what is sometimes called reform, and for the next few years pretty much ran the island

that now amounts to Haiti and the Dominican Republic. Maine sea captains, who traded with much profit in
the West Indies, always called the island San Domingo.
It was discovered by Columbus in 1492, and then the
Spaniards moved in and enslaved all the native American Indians. This led to the extinction of the Indians,
after which black slaves were imported from Africa. By
the time England and France got to wrangling over the
place, the population had squared away to three kinds
of people.

The landowners had come to be known as *colons*, a
word also used in French Canada for the settlers. Then
there were the Negroes, as then called—the freed slaves.
Third were the inbreeds and other mixtures that came
from the Spaniards and the Indians, plus help from the
general neighborhood and anybody else ready and willing, and they got dubbed *mulattoes* whether they were
or not. Seems the colons tried to ride things out, but
the freed slaves got uppity, and the mulattoes felt supe-
rior, and things got into a situation where this Pierre
Dominique Toussaint L'Ouverture was able to organize
a revolution and get control of the island. He became
known as the "Black Napoleon," and had himself
crowned Emperor of San Domingo.

Toussaint L'Ouverture wasn't exactly the high-prin-
cipled character William Wordsworth put into his son-
net—Wordsworth seemed to think he was a kindly
liberator and a pillar of probity. He was, rather, a butcher
and a despot, and a low-level intellect. He had a jutting
jaw like a Fisher snowplow, and a receding brow that
pinched off his brain. As to being a "soldier," he rather
playacted at that, swaggering and bossy, and sporting
magnificent uniforms with epaulets that stuck out a yard.
He wore tricorn hats to make him look like Napoleon.

His atrocities were fierce. He was, in a few words, a deep-jungle prehistoric apeman, a cruel, untutored barbarian. However, he was in control of San Domingo, favoring the French and detesting the English, and up until just bout that time, 1793, anybody from the Province of Maine was English. Two Maine ship captains, Asa Clapp and Bill McClellan, witnessed the cold massacre of every other white person on the island, and luckily escaped to come home and tell about it. Their story discouraged trade, and Maine boats stopped taking cargo to Haiti and San Domingo.

But at just about that time the United States of America began to seem promising, and now we come to Captain Walter Prout, earliest of the Freeport Prouts, who meditated on this situation down in San Domingo, where certain goods were needed and certain others were available but nobody cared to venture by. Toussaint L'Ouverture was indeed a bully, but Captain Prout was venturesome, and Captain Prout reasoned that a bit of down-Maine chicanery (the Maine word is "snedricks") might turn a penny in spite of the way things were. He accordingly took his brig *Gerfalcon* to Bangor and loaded her with $7,000 worth of good Penobscot white pine (plus the usual deckload of "scoots"), and big as Billie-be-damned he dropped down to San Domingo Harbor and cast anchor.

What happened is exactly what he expected would happen—he was immediately arrested, his crew cast in jail, and his vessel and cargo confiscated to the personal purposes of Pierre Dominique Toussaint L'Ouverture, the Emperor.

In those days every deep-water vessel carried a "sea letter." It was a form letter asking foreign nations to be friendly, and if any problem arose in a foreign port the letter was intended to ease matters. It was a "To whom it may concern" sort of thing, and offered no assurance that any prince, nabob, potentate would pay it any heed if he didn't care to. Captain Walter Prout had always carried a sea letter, but the one he had now was in mint condition. The United States of America had just lately issued its sea letters, and Captain Prout had picked his up at the customs house in Bangor just before he sailed with his *Gerfalcon*. The letter was signed by our brand-new president, G. Washington.

And Captain Walter Prout was perfectly aware that Pierre Dominique Toussaint L'Ouverture was a fanatical admirer of General Washington. Toussaint L'Ouverture even had uniforms just like Washington's, and when he was wearing one he would buckle-swash his sword about and make believe he was teaching Lord Cornwallis a lesson or two. So Captain Prout made no resistance to the seizure of his vessel and cargo, to the arrest of his men, and to his own rude detention. He merely asked that he might have a word with His Excellency the Great Emperor, inasmuch as he had a message for him from the President of the United States. He artfully dropped the name of George Washington.

A hulk of a huge black sergeant (as Captain Prout's log had it) carried the message to Toussaint L'Ouverture, who was at once overwhelmed and asked that Captain Prout be fetched immediately.

Captain Prout found Toussaint L'Ouverture in full Napoleonic uniform, surrounded by his colorful elite guard, reclining in a hammock, attended by his cup bearer, and being fanned by a retainer in silk breeches and velvet waistcoat. Captain Prout was not sure just how he should approach the monarch, but he stuck out his warm Yankee hand and shook. Toussaint L'Ouverture used only French, a tongue Captain Prout knew nothing about, so the huge sergeant became the interpreter, and the exercises commenced. Captain Prout opened his sea letter and began to read. He did not, you can bet, start off by saying, "To whom it may concern . . ." Instead, he read, "To your most illustrious sovereignty . . ." And as he read on, he interpolated as he saw fit, and his sea letter became an extremely complimentary communication directly from President George Washington to Emperor P. D. T. L'Ouverture, friend to friend. Toussaint L'Ouverture was delighted.

So the emperor asked what cargo Captain Prout had brought, and also what he would like to have in return. The crew members were released, and the *Gerfalcon* was moved to wharfage for discharge of $7,000 worth of Maine pine lumber. Wharfage fees were waived. Then the *Gerfalcon* was loaded with sugar and coffee, and the log recorded that no brig ever took on, ton for ton, such cargo. The crew's beds were piled with bags of coffee, and the men made shift on the decks. The profits from this voyage went over $80,000 and Captain Prout returned to San Domingo several times before the real Napoleon, in France, had Toussaint L'Ouverture arrested, and the monopoly of Captain Walter Prout sadly came to an end. He was not chagrined, however, at this end to his prosperity, but simply retired home to Maine and became a philanthropist.

21

A consideration of what three hogsheads of dried beans would mean in the economy of the New World in the very early years of the seventeenth century, with the thought that sometimes the historians miss the point.

That historians seldom know beans is readily shown by a glance at the year 1613. That was a pinpoint year, and pinpoint years are scarce in history books. Well, we don't know just when the Goths left Sweden, or when the Incas built Cuzco, but we do know that 1613 was the year that Maine stopped being French and became English. The same thing happened to the cow, and the beans are important, too.

The King of France had every right by discovery and exploration to give Acadia to the Sieur de Monts. Acadia was the Micmac Indian name for the tribal lands in

Maine, New Brunswick, and Nova Scotia, and in 1602 de Monts came with some settlers and took up his property. Shortly, there were posts at Port Royal, Ste. Croix Island, and St. Sauveur on Mount Desert Island. Next de Monts signed off to Lady Guerchville, and she prevailed on Henry IV to confirm the grant to her and to extend it so she owned everything between Philadelphia and Labrador, and as far inland as she cared to claim. They didn't know yet just where the Pacific Ocean might be, but wherever it was, that was her limit. Good snatch of land.

Notice that this was well before the English made any pretense at colonization, and the best we had were seasonal fishery stations off on Maine islands. When King James of England bestowed his "Virginia," his grant set up two companies to further settlements and trade. One was the London Company, which got "South Virginia," and the other was the Plymouth Company, which got Maine, or "North Virginia." As for Maine, King James was giving away land that was already well in the possession of the French, and to which he had no more right at that time than he did to the Vatican. Then followed the Jamestown settlement and the attempt to settle at Popham here in Maine. The Popham effort fizzled, and the people went back to England.

Now to the beans. When de Monts set up shop on Ste. Croix Island, near present Calais, he and his men had a rough time, but they didn't fizzle. A couple of years later a vessel came up the Ste. Croix River, making in from the ocean, and she was in trouble. She was short on supplies. Yes, the folks at Ste. Croix Island could help, and they fixed the ship up and she sailed on. Now, these folks gave the ship three hogsheads of dry beans. If any historian knew anything about clearing land, tilling the soil, planting, cultivating, harvesting, and then threshing and winnowing beans, he would pause right there and dwell on the information. The English at Jamestown weren't all that well off; the English at Popham would find they couldn't grow anything and would quit. But here are these Frenchmen well able to meet their own needs, and rolling in wealth to the extent that they could let three hogsheads of beans go.

That's a lot of beans.

It indicates a prosperity we shouldn't pass over lightly. It establishes beyond further question the control of the land and the secure footing the French had on it. But instead of taking notice of such suzerainty, the historians dwell on how somebody put up a cross and things like that. Indeed, that's just what they did say—that Lady Guerchville's colonists, sixty in all, "planted" a cross on Mount Desert Island and called their village St. Sauveur. It was upon St. Sauveur that the righteous English were to wreak havoc and change history.

Two Jesuit priests—missionaries—had left Port Royal and come over to Mount Desert Island to bring Christian light to the savages. They already had their huts and a small chapel when Lady Guerchville's colonists joined them. They were Fathers Biard and Massé. It didn't take long for the new arrivals to set up cabins, to clear land, and make drying racks ready for codfish. And news of this "encroachment" came to the good burghers of Virginia, and they were wroth. It wasn't because these Frenchmen were crowding in and the neighborhood was going to pot; it was because they were competition about the cod. The good burghers, who enjoy a comfortable place in the history books, were not above skulduggery. They saw nothing snide about having a villain do good deeds, so they fitted out "Captain" Samuel Argal with eleven ships, mounting fourteen competent cannon, and sent along sixty soldiers to help the captain if he ran into trouble. Captain Argal was a pirate, pure and simple, but neither pure nor simple. He sailed for Maine.

The Frenchmen at St. Sauveur didn't know this army or this navy was coming, and on that bright summer day in 1613 they were minding their own business, cutting firewood, splitting fish, hoeing beans and corn, and Fathers Biard and Massé were circulating about in their spiritual fashion to encourage and comfort. It was about as pretty a day as Mount Desert Island had seen.

Just then a cannon ball ripped into the village, followed by its delayed sound of explosion, and everybody looked up to see Captain Argal's fleet of eleven ships approaching. Now Captain Argal gave them the other thirteen guns, and at nigh point-blank range this tore apart most of the dwellings, and also broke one of Father Massé's legs. The French did have a couple of ships of their own anchored, but unmanned, and Father Biard leaves us a few words: "All, save Father Massé, sought haven in the forest, but one of us, being braver than the rest, went aboard one of our ships and touched off the guns, making them to speak as loudly as the British." But as something of a wistful afterthought, Father Biard goes on, "But not taking aim, his barrage came to naught." The English swept on, and with gallantry Captain Argal captured an empty and undefended village. And now we see why the good burghers of Jamestown sent so many ships when one or two might have sufficed.

Captain Argal stole everything he could find, and that included the cow. In the righteous annals of the Jamestown settlement we learn that Jamestown had the first milch cow in the colonies. This was the cow Captain

Argal stole at St. Sauveur, and as this cow didn't understand any English, Captain Argal took Father Biard to
Jamestown so he could handle the cow. Father Biard
thus spent some time at Jamestown, where he wrote his
version of the attack on St. Sauveur; he stayed until the
cow learned a little English. Having reduced St. Sauveur, Captain Argal now moved on to Port Royal and
repeated his success in the same way. Then he took his
plunder to Jamestown and received a hero's welcome.
Which pretty much took care of Acadia, and served to
turn the efforts of France up the St. Lawrence River
and into Canada. The pinpoint date is 1613. Just suppose if he who was braver than the rest, the Frenchman
who ran aboard the boat, had paused to take aim, and
his barrage had blown Captain Argal to hell-and-gone.
. . . Just suppose on that beautiful Mount Desert morning that things had gone the other way. . . . We would
have a very different Maine today. Ah, oui!

22

An effort to retell the improbabilities of Maine's "Aroostook War" so they make sense, along with a deserved deflation of the great Daniel Webster, and a few words about Hiram Smith, who lost his life.

There's an old history of the State of Maine that begins the story of the "Aroostook War" on page 430, and has a picture of the state insane hospital at Augusta on page 431. This is very good reporting. The Aroostook War remains the world's most amusing conflict to date, and its strategy could well have come out of that hospital. The Tweedledum-Tweedledee exercise gained some respect because it ended in the fine Webster-Ashburton Treaty, with wise old Daniel Webster coming out of the scrimmage smelling like a rose. Stephen Vincent Benét notwithstanding, Daniel Webster made a ninny of himself and foolishly gave away a goodly hunk of Maine—sending Lord Ashburton home to England chuckling away to himself.

That part of Maine and New Brunswick where the St. John River makes the boundary is known as "The Valley." It has always been French, but not the French of Québec. Instead, its settlers came after "le grand dérangement," when the British uprooted the Acadian French in Nova Scotia and dispersed them. Not all the Acadians went to Louisiana with Henry Wadsworth Longfellow, and some of them moved up the St. John River and took up the good meadowland along the St. John which is now termed The Valley. The Valley was then remote, and in a way still is, and it certainly was when the wonderful Aroostook War was thought up. The Acadians there had no love for the English, and didn't know too much about the United States of America. That dispersement was in 1755, so the Acadians in The Valley were well settled before there was any United States of America.

The treaty after the Revolutionary War, in 1783, divided The Valley down the middle—half Maine and half New Brunswick. At that time England didn't see too far ahead and didn't consider that Maine would jut up into the map and cut off, say, Halifax from, say, Montreal. Neither did the United States, because it was going to be some time—the middle 1800s—before English-speaking people moved up into Aroostook and began planting potatoes. So the Acadians went along in their remote and unrelated way—sort of neither hay nor grass.

It wasn't until the end of the War of 1812 that England knew she had goofed on her trans-Canada route. She now claimed both sides of the St. John, and more, too, but there was no great excitement about this at the time. It was a few years later that Madawaska, Maine's most northerly town, wanted to send a representative down to legislature in Augusta, and the English realized such representation would jeopardize their claim. Constables from New Brunswick came across the river and made a nuisance of themselves at peaceful meetings in the Madawaska parish hall. But nothing like hostility broke out until 1837. Governor Robert P. Dunlap of Brunswick was in office at Augusta in 1834 when the fuse was lit.

The United States Treasury, from a period of prosperity after the War of 1812, had a surplus, and Congress voted to distribute it among the states. When it came to Maine, the town of Madawaska was due to get its share, and Governor Dunlap sent his agent up-country with a purse of funds. After an arduous trip, the officer got to Madawaska, and was immediately arrested by a New Brunswick constable who hustled him to Fredericton and into a cold, clammy uncomfortable cell in the York County jail. There was a language problem, since the officer didn't speak French. If the Madawaskans had understood his mission, they'd have intervened. Even today, you go into Madawaska and offer money, and somebody will readily take it and express his thanks.

The high sheriff at Fredericton was leery of all this, thinking maybe the constable had been hasty, and he was afraid he might be mixed up in a nasty international mess, so he sent the officer back to Madawaska and asked the constable to apologize. Thereupon the officer now accomplished his mission and gave the money to the town of Madawaska, since which time most Madawaskans have been friendly to the United States.

But now tidings of this came to the governor of New Brunswick, name of Harvey, who cried foul. He said the distribution of the money was no more than a bribe to make the Madawaskans shift their allegiance, and he would not permit an American agent thus to step on British soil. He ordered the agent to be rearrested, and once more the poor soul was in the pokey in Fredericton. Governor Harvey must have been a bit slow, as he knew very well what "allegiance" the Madawaskans had for the British bruisers who had run them out of Grand Pré.

So now word of this comes to Governor Robert P. Dunlop of Maine, whose term of office had hitherto been quiet and relaxing, and he had just at that very moment remarked that it would be exciting if something should happen. His joy was unbounded. He leaped up and in a fiery extemporaneous speech stated without fear of successful contradiction that the sacred soil of Maine had been contaminated by alien foot, violated by the heel of tyranny, and he, for one, by the Old Harry, was not going to lie back and take it sitting down. He called upon the militia to be ready at an instant's notice. He was some worked up, he was. But President Martin Van Buren, down in Washington, took a calmer view, and suggested to Governor Harvey over in New Brunswick if they'd just let the agent go, it would probably spare Governor Dunlap a heart seizure. The emergency was thus over, and the "Battle of Madawaska" ended. But there had been considerable marching up and down on both sides of the St. John River. This amused the Madawaskans.

Just how the king of the Netherlands got into this is conjectural. The British were now claiming all of Maine above forty-six degrees north latitude, and the argument boiled down to which of two lines was the right one. The king of the Netherlands, name of William, agreed to arbitrate this, but instead of deciding which line was the right line, he came up with an altogether different line all his own. This solution had no sympathy in England or in the United States, but it added amusement to living in Madawaska.

But at one time there was some small thought about accepting the line of Dutch King William. Perhaps Congress, down in Washington, was fed up with all the clatter out of Maine. Anyway, Congress did offer Maine a million acres of public land out in Michigan if the state would just simmer down and accept King William's suggestion and give Madawaska to the English. This offer was turned down because nobody in Madawaska wanted to go and live in Michigan. By this time our governor was Edward Kent of Bangor, and he sent General Wool to see that our defenses to the east and north were adequate. General Wool did this from a room in the Huston House at Mattawamkeag—he got the place confused with Madawaska. The phase of the war that followed had to do with the no-man's strip between the Maine and New Brunswick contentions.

Both sides, thinking maybe the land would soon go to the other, began plundering the timber. The English had an advantage, because the St. John River flowed into New Brunswick and they could float their logs away. Now the Maine legislature authorized Sheriff Strickland of Kennebec County to raise a force of two hundred volunteers to go up and drive the dirty English back where they belonged. He turned this veritable army, consisting of unemployed wood choppers rather than soldiers, over to Captain Stover Rines, who left Bangor on February 5, 1839, and reached Masardis on the eighth.

This was good time in those days, and by an initial, and surprise, assault Captain Rines captured seven teams of horses and three teamsters all named Cyr.

Flushed with success, Rines now advanced to the mouth of the Little Madawaska River, which is a tributary of the Aroostook River, which is a tributary of the St. John River. Here a bunch of rude New Brunswickers met him with axes and frying pans, and Captain Stover Rines was captured, put into a sleigh, and jingled off to Fredericton to the same old jail. His men retreated to Masardis, where Sheriff Strickland greeted them and asked what happened. Then the sheriff returned to Augusta, took a room at the Augusta House, and reported to Governor Kent, who promised to do something shortly.

Having Captain Rines as proof, Governor Harvey of New Brunswick now complained that *his* sovereign territory had been invaded by foreign rascals, issued a proclamation, and ordered up a thousand militia to advance against said rascals. Governor Kent, even though it was a Sunday morning, responded by sending fifty volunteers from Augusta, who advanced at triple-trot to meet the thousand New Brunswickers. At this Governor Harvey sent a message to Governor Kent saying he would occupy the disputed area at all costs. This was war!

It was 1839, and the Maine legislature had come into existence only in 1820, so this was its first brush with conflict. Eight hundred thousand dollars were appropriated to fight the New Brunswickers, and an order was passed to raise 10,343 men from the militia, to be ready for immediate action. Nobody has ever explained this particular number, but Bill Pattangall once suggested it was, at that time, the total enrollment.

It was at this time that the "Military Road" was built through the woods to Houlton, and the two forts were

laid up that were named for Governors Kent and Fairfield—giving names to the present towns of Fort Kent
and Fort Fairfield.

General Bachelder, assigned to command this levy,
made ready to advance, but it was now midwinter and
the men were all in summer uniforms. Everything had
to wait until new uniforms could arrive. The historians
are careful to tell us that the men received bright red
shirts and pea-green jackets, but neglect to tell about
their pants. The new uniforms were adequately warm,
but it was thirty below zero when General Bachelder
led his troops up the Military Road into Aroostook.
Nobody was happy about that.

Congress in Washington now rallied, and authorized
the president to raise fifty thousand troops to help the
Mainers whip the New Brunswickers. Congress also
raised ten million dollars to support them. Shortly,
General Scott arrived in Augusta and took a suite at the
Augusta House, from which he viewed the situation and
pondered. He had thirty thousand troops he could
deploy, but he rightly felt it was too cold in Maine to
go out and command them. Accordingly, he took a conciliatory course and persuaded Governors Fairfield and
Harvey to postpone a battle and leave the question to
diplomacy. Both agreed, and this was the end of hostil-
ities.

Then came the meeting between Lord Alexander
Baring Ashburton of England and United States Secretary of State Daniel Webster. Daniel Webster delivered several major speeches and recalled the old days
when he was tedding hay back on the New Hampshire
farm, and Lord Ashburton nursed his brandy and soda
and kept saying, "Hyar, hyar!" As a result, Daniel
Webster gave away a great many square miles of Maine
with their virgin stands of prime upland lumber, and

Lord Ashburton assured himself of a generous pension, which, they say, is still in effect. There have been those who feel we should have listened to King William of the Netherlands.

This Aroostook War has been called the "bloodless war." In spite of the time and the number of soldiers involved, including sheriffs, agents, governors, choppers and sawyers, farmers and smugglers, there was but one casualty. Some say his name was Hiram Smith. Others say it wasn't. There are stories, myths, and legends, and whichever tale you tell, somebody will dispute you. His grave is up along the Military Road, and some say he was buried where he fell. It's just about where the army began its trudge through the snow, leaving the kindly climate of Maine and heading into the incredible frigidity of Aroostook, "The County." There he lies, for all may go to see. One story says he took a dip to cleanse and refresh himself, and thus caught a cold. In the middle of the winter? Nobody ever got dirty enough for that. Another is that he fell in a pond and died of pneumonia. Another is that there was nothing the matter with him, but he just folded up from the idea of going to Aroostook.

The best story, be it history or not, is that he got run over by a supply wagon. From time to time somebody in Howland will add that "he broke his leg and they had to shoot him." But does it matter? Historians like to dangle their degrees and insist on accuracy. Pee-shaw! The whole point is that the poor devil died in a humiliating manner that had nothing whatever to do with the consequences of battle. His name, his rank, and his serial number are not important. He epitomizes the Aroostook War. *He was its only casualty.*

Historian's note: Along about 1987, somebody went

to look at the lonely tombstone of Hiram Smith, and found that it had been removed. Since Route 95 was constructed, there has been less traffic over the old Military Road, so nobody visits the spot often, and nobody knows how long the stone had been gone before it was missed. Possibly its removal is a fitting epilogue to the total foolishness of the Aroostook War, but who would steal a tombstone? Later, while this book was in preparation for the printer: The person(s) unknown who pilfered the lonely tombstone of Private Hiram Smith from the Haynesville Woods may have felt remorse, for in September of 1989 a new tombstone, not at all like the one that had been stolen, was set on the base of the first—again, by person(s) unknown. Hiram Smith, again, was plagued by his infernal bad luck. The new stone says he fought in the "Indian wars." He did not, but when you ponder on Hiram Smith, does it matter?

Private Hiram Smith's new tombstone

23

A few words about the great
"King" LaCroix, the Beauceman
who outdid Paul Bunyan, and
how he operated the pulpwood
railroad at "The Tramway" at
Eagle Lake on the Allagash
River; he was "jarret noir."

Fortunately, many stories about Edward "King" LaCroix
are untrue. The same may be said of Paul Bunyan. For
example, when M. LaCroix went down to Philadelphia
to buy two steam locomotives from the Pennsylvania
Railroad, it is said that he got off the train and asked
the taxi driver to take him to "the best hovel in town."
The taxi man understood him to say "hotel," which is
exactly what M. LaCroix meant but not what he said.
Back in the Maine woods, where M. LaCroix was already
a bigger legend than Paul Bunyan, a hovel was the
building of a sprawling lumber camp where the horses

were housed. It could, therefore, be a shelter and a place to pass a night, and that's what M. LaCroix, who was never proficient in English, was looking for.

Being at that time (so the legend runs) garbed in the felt boots and rubbers (larrigans) and the heavy garments of a Maine lumber camp, M. LaCroix was viewed askance by the receptionist at the best hotel in Philadelphia, who was unaware that beneath the rough clothing was a man of several self-made millions, and one with the complete confidence of a consortium of Montreal Bankers. The bankers had just financed the railroad for which M. LaCroix desired two locomotives. M. LaCroix signed the register as representing the Madawaska Company, and asked when supper would be ready.

At that moment it was 1926 back in Maine, and the Madawaska Company was building that thirteen-mile railway from Eagle Lake on the Allagash waters over to Umbazookskus Lake on the West Branch of the Penobscot River. This railway would haul millions of cords of pulpwood over the height of land toward the Great Northern Paper Company mill at Millinocket. Several hundred men had been working to build the railway, which means that M. LaCroix was not only in the railroad business, but he was also in the food business. The cookshacks where his chefs fed the assemblage of appetites would baffle the chefs of the finest hotel in Philadelphia. When M. LaCroix spoke of supper, he meant supper.

He dined sumptuously that evening. He had the double tenderloin steak with onions and mushroom, a baked potato, and topped off with the apple pie and ice cream. He settled back contentedly when he had finished, and whipped out a Canadian ten-dollar bill to reward the waiter who had given him such good care. Then M.

LaCroix arose, and as all good choppers in every good Maine lumber camp always do, he picked up his dishes and carried them to the sink. This amused the pot wallopers in the kitchen, and M. LaCroix affably shook hands with them and offered them jobs up at Eagle Lake if they ever cared to make a change.

The next day M. LaCroix kept his appointment with the Pennsylvania Railroad people, and he told them he was down from Maine to learn if he could buy two freight locomotives for his railroad. He did his best to explain that the Eagle Lake & West Branch Railroad would carry pulpwood from the Allagash to the Penobscot. Not knowing anything about pulpwood, the Pennsy people were amused at his broken English, and nodded—yes, they had some obsolete steam equipment they could offer. What did he have in mind? M. LaCroix pointed out the office window towards the marshaling yards, where a number of engines were at work.

"H'I'll tak dat wan, an' dat wan."

"Oh? Why those two?"

"Because dey's run-NING."

Some stories say Mr. LaCroix drew out his wallet and laid cash for his two locomotives on the desk, shook hands, and left at once for Maine—the engines to be delivered over Canadian Pacific rails to Lac Frontière, Québec. There they would be dismantled and taken by Lombard log haulers to Eagle Lake, by way of the Nine Mile Bridge across the St. John River. (That bridge was never nine miles long—it was nine miles from Lac Frontière.)

Fortunately, these adventures of M. LaCroix in Philadelphia are not true. His two steam locomotives are still at Eagle Lake; one of them bears the letters N.Y.C. & H.R., and the other one is a 2–8–0 from the Rutland

Railroad. There is a bare possibility that Edward "King' LaCroix was never in Philadelphia.

The place to see these two abandoned locomotives is now called "The Tramway," at Eagle Lake. The spot has been important in Maine lumbering history for going on two centuries. Since the Allagash River flows northerly and eventually turns into New Brunswick, that river was of no use to Maine lumbering interests to the south. A scheme to dam the waters of Allagash Stream at Chamberlain Lake, thus raising the level of Chamberlain so there would be flowage by way of Telos Lake towards the East Branch of the Penobscot, seemed feasible, and work began.

The scheme included a canal to be dug at Telos. But the Allagash flows into the St. John, and the St. John was important to Canadians; as a result, the loss of that much water occasioned the "Telos War." Several times the Canadians came up the Allagash and put "the powduh" (dynamite) to the lock dam at Chamberlain. This released enough water so there was a great surge, and the Canadians would push their bateaux onto the crest and ride hell-bent back to New Brunswick. The Mainers never did catch them in the act. But choppers and river drivers who hired out to work in the area well understood that at any moment they might be soldiers rather than ax men, and there were times when heads got thwacked. Mostly, however, the Telos War was a replay of the Bloodless Aroostook War, and Lock Dam at Chamberlain Lake is still in place and still sending Allagash Stream into the East Branch, rather than into the Allagash River.

As the twentieth century came up, a better scheme took shape. An endless cable device of tremendous dimensions would take logs from Eagle Lake over the hump and dump them in Chamberlain Lake. Men went to work. The steel for this device, to be known as the tramway, was prefabbed in New Jersey and shipped by rail to Greenville. Then it went by boat (and in winter by sleds on the ice) to Northeast Carry, to be taken the rest of the way by horse or tractor. The distance of the tramway was three thousand feet, so the endless cable came to six thousand feet, weighing fourteen tons. The cable, rolled up, was supposed to arrive at Eagle Lake in one piece, but it had to be cut for transport, and then at considerable expense a wire splicer had to be brought from New Jersey to put it together again. There were 4,800 $\frac{7}{8}$-inch bolts to hold the lugs to the cable, and they arrived from New Jersey with the threads too short. Every bolt had to be removed and more threading cut with hand dies, and then replaced and taken up. This took time and cost money, but it was still cheaper than sending the foolish bolts back to New Jersey.

The tramway had its doubters and its troubles, but when at last it was ready to turn, it worked. A steam engine on the Chamberlain Lake end huffed and puffed to get the cable, with all its lugs, moving, but once the engine got the sprocket wheel up to 250 rpm, the tramway proved efficient. It operated from 1901 through six seasons and successfully moved well over a hundred million board feet of prime timber.

When the 1920s came along, Edward LaCroix was already prominent in Maine's north woods. He was born at St. Georges, Beauce County, Quebec, a native "jarret noir" and a true "canuck." From the beginnings of Maine's north woods lumbering, French-speaking Canadians have been indispensable. The first to come over the line to earn good money as "choppers" brought with them their own word—"canuck." Derived from

Montaignais Indian, it means a stranger, a visitor, even a foreigner. Compare the German *Fremde*. The canuck was "from away." In the beginning the word had no flavor of mockery, but when later migrations of Quebeckers came down to work in the Maine cotton mills, from other parts of Quebec, the term was resented.

On the other hand, the term "jarret noir" was mocking from the beginning. The *jarret* is the back of the knee, the shank of a horse. When early Beauce County farmers drove their wagons into Quebec City to trade, they could be identified by the rich, black Beauce County mud on the shanks of their horses. Children would taunt, "Voici les jarrets noirs!" and the folks from Beauce didn't like that. But time mellowed things, and today a person born in Beauce County will wear a gold medallion on a chain about his neck with pride. The canuck and the jarret noir played big roles in Maine woods history. After all, they live closer to those north woods than the Yankees do!

So King LaCroix was contracting to cut and deliver pulpwood to the downstate paper mills, and Great Northern Paper Company approached him about moving wood from the Eagle Lake and St. John areas towards Millinocket. The route would be somewhat like that which occasioned the Telos War, and that of the abandoned tramway. LaCroix and "The Northern" negotiated in good faith, and neither anticipated the great financial disturbance that would bring on the Roosevelt depression. But all at once the crash came, and the terms of the contract became extremely favorable to LaCroix and just about ruinous to Great Northern. Tactfully, The Northern suggested renegotiating the contract, setting a new rate per cord that took the depression into consideration. At this, King LaCroix asked to be excused while he stepped outside to laugh. Great Northern thus bought extremely expensive wood and King LaCroix was glad. In the end, Northern rode the thing out and turned a corporate profit, but around Millinocket King LaCroix was mentioned with distaste.

Meantime he had consulted the Montreal bankers and was out-Pauling Bunyan. The rails were laid for the Eagle Lake & West Branch Railroad, his locomotives arrived, and one day the first trainload of Eagle Lake pulpwood moved to Umbazookskus Lake. It took three hours for each round trip, ten cars of pulpwood to a train. A hundred thousand cords of pulpwood floating in Eagle Lake; each week 6,500 cord were moved to Umbazookskus. The railroad operated from August 1, 1927, through the season of 1931, when King LaCroix abandoned his railroad and moved on to other projects. He earned his nickname of King, and he deserves the legends about him—true or not.

The trip to Philadelphia aside, there is one good King LaCroix story that is true, and men are still living who remember the incident. The great man got caught up in the immutable Maine rule that lumber camp meals are eaten in silence. Conversation can lead to differences of opinion, and these to discussions and arguments. Arguments lead to fights, and fights disturb the decorum of the table. Of the dining hall in a lumber camp it is said, "Dis room if for h'eat—you wanna talk, you go on de bed-ROOM." The cook, undisputed boss of the cook-shack, enforced this rule, and there was no appeal to any higher authority.

So King LaCroix came into the cookshack at Nine Mile camp one time for a meal while on his way to Eagle Lake, and he began whispering to his foreman about business matters. This certainly violated the rule against

talk at table, but King LaCroix owned that whole she-
bang, and every rule has its exception. But not that rule.
As the men ate, the voices of LaCroix and his foreman
could be heard, and the choppers looked at the cook,
wondering what he would do.

The cook did his duty. He stepped up behind King
LaCroix and suggested the conversation be put in recess
until the meal was over, or be continued "h'outside."
King LaCroix, concerned about what his foreman was
saying, waved the cook off and continued to talk.

That did it. "Dis my room, you shut h'up!" yelled
the cook, and he grabbed LaCroix by the collar and jerked
him to the door. He hove LaCroix through the door
into the snowbank, and then he threw the foreman out,
too. He shouted, "Now, you talk!"

There were no repercussions. Neither Owner LaCroix
nor Boss MacIver took umbrage. The cook was right.
They came in, brushing snow, and sat down to finish
their food in silence. Then they went "on de bed-
ROOM" to resume their conversation.

Remains of the Eagle Lake & West Branch Railroad
can be found in the region, everything where it was left,
and the two locomotives are at "The Tramway" at Eagle
Lake, monuments to King LaCroix, who was as real as
Paul Bunyan was not. Canoeists going down the Allagash in the pleasant days of their summer outings look
at those engines in disbelief, unable to visualize and
imagine the gigantic pulpwood operation that brought
these improbable monsters into the far Maine woods.

24

How a goodwife in the still of
night heard a stick of dynamite
explode but didn't think
much about it; and how the
local banker turned detective
and brought the bank robber
to justice because his
horse interfered.

Sometime during the evening of September 22nd, 1867,
Mrs. Clarissa Babcock Newington[1] was sitting up late
to finish a doily for tomorrow's church sale, and her
close attention to her work was interrupted by an explosion. It wasn't too far away, and it might have blown
off the front porch. Mrs. Newington looked up from
her work in wonder about what could make such a
dreadful noise in the middle of the night, when all good

1. This is a fictitious name, because of the sensitivity of her descendants.
Mrs. Newington seemed a trifle slow on the uptake.

Christian souls should be abed if they had nothing to keep them up, as she had, and then she turned back to resume her needlework. This should be inserted in the annals of humankind to show that the female intellect is not at its best after supper, for Mrs. Newington lived in the center of Norway village, just across from the Lee Mixer General Store on the main street. After Mrs. Newington finished the doily she retired, being careful not to waken her sleeping huisband, and it didn't occur to her to rouse him and report that something very like a bomb had taken place. She didn't tell him about it at breakfast, either, but gave him the doily and asked him to drop it off at the house of the committee chairlady on his way to work.[2]

Otherwise, the solution of the Great Norway Savings Bank Robbery might have been at hand within minutes of the time the thieves blew the safe with a stick of dynamite. In those days banking was in its formative stage in Maine communities, and the Norway Savings Bank was barely a year old. It was so new, indeed, that it didn't yet have its own counting house, but rented space in the Lee Mixer General Store just across the street from the Newington home where Mrs. Newington heard the dynamite go off but didn't think it was important. As a consequence, the robbery was not discovered until the following morning[3] when Lee Mixer came to open his store. He found the door of the safe over on a molasses barrel and a rear window of the store bereft, ajar, and derelict.

Surmising theft, Mr. Mixer hurried to find Charles C. Sanderson, a lawyer and trustee of the Norway Sav-

2. Mr. Newington operated a square-bar mill.
3. September 23rd.

ings Bank. Mr. Sanderson was accustomed to bankers' hours and was lingering over his eggs and bacon, but he pulled on his pants and hurried to the scene. There, as had Mr. Mixer, he concluded the bank had been robbed. And being a trustee of the bank as well as a lawyer, he at once had the unnerving thought that somebody might suggest an "inside job" and he might be erroneously considered the thief. Innocent as he was, this thought caused him to become eager to ferret out the real thief, and Lawyer Sanderson thus became a regular Perry Mason[4] or Sherlock Holmes.[5] He talked with just about everybody in town that forenoon, and somebody told him there had been a strange horse and buggy in town, and somebody else said he'd heard a horse stomping in the sheds behind the Congregational Church.[6]

Squire Sanderson went to look, and in the horse sheds behind the church he found hoofprints that were new enough to have been made just the night before. He surmised that the thief, or thieves, had hidden the animal and buggy in the sheds while they entered the store

4. An odd series of happenstances. Dr. Charles A. Stephens of Norway was already writing his "Old Squire Stories" for the *Youth's Companion*, published in Boston by the Perry Mason Company. Erle Stanley Gardner grew up in the Boston area, and took the name of the publisher for his lawyer-detective who now reminds us of Attorney Sanderson. It's a small world.

5. Sherlock Holmes, a detective of some note in England.

6. Horsesheds. All community churches of the day had sheltering sheds where parishioners "stood" their horses during services. To hear a horse stomping in a horseshed except while church was holding devotions would excite curiosity. Sometimes during town meetings (held in the same meeting house) members who had funny ideas and wouldn't go along with the majority were invited to step out to the horseshed where they could be reasoned with. Nothing dire—some of his fellow citizens would explain things to him until he was amenable, and this democratic process was known as "horseshedding." After being horseshedded, a man would return to the meeting and show better sense.

through the back window and touched off the dynamite. If so, the hoofprints were very important, and he stooped to examine them. He noticed that one shoe of the horse was the kind farriers made to prevent a horse from "interfering." Now and then an otherwise sound horse would have a shinbone twisted a mite so he would kick himself in the other leg every time he stepped. This would bring tears to his eyes and make him less useful in a swap. The blacksmith could shoe him to stop this if he knew how, and in this instance the blacksmith knew how and he did. The odd shoe on that horse was odd enough so it could be tracked anywhere so long as a shower didn't wash things out. Squire Sanderson had his clue—the rest was to trace the horse and the man who drove him.

He traced the horse to Portland[7] where a liveryman said yes, he had rented the horse with the interfering shoe to a man who gave the name of Truman F. Young of Nashua, New Hampshire, and that the horse had been returned in good shape and paid for. Lawyer Sanderson then took a train to Boston and turned the matter over to a detective agency. The game was afoot!

In due time this Truman Young was apprehended, and when convicted was sentenced to nine years at hard labor in the Maine State Prison at Thomaston. Soon after he was comfortably installed in this hospitable institution he decided to "sing," and he said he had masterminded this caper and carried it out with the help of two gentlemen from New York City, one of whom was an old hand at dynamite. His astute handling of "The Case of the Interfering Horse" won Squire Sanderson some recognition, and for a long time his reputation

7. Portland. Portland was incorporated a city in 1833.

deterred many a New Yorker who would otherwise come to Maine to rob and steal. He left the Norway Savings Bank in good shape, so it was soon able to buy a new safe and move to its own location, where it prospered until today it has substantial assets and a fine reputation throughout that part of Maine. It is interesting that the old Mixer store later became the offices of the weekly Norway *Independent-Democrat*, a paper rightly esteemed for its whimsical editorials and as the place where Charles Farrar Browne learned to set type back before he became Artemus Ward.[8]

8. The thieves got $3,946.70.

25

Some words about the Maine
privateers in the War of 1812,
and the curious fashion in which
a "letter of marque" was caused
to justify the "prize" of a herd
of up-country cattle on its way
into Canada.

The difference between a privateer and a pirate is quickly
stated: the privateer has a license to steal. The pirate is
on his own, engaging in his depredations in a private
and personal pursuit, and if he gets caught they string
him up. The privateer does the same work, but is sponsored by his government so that he is respectable, and
if he doesn't get caught they give him a congressional
medal. During the War of 1812 a good many Maine
men earned good money being privateers. As for the
morality involved, the barely new United States of
America didn't have much of a navy, and by issuing

"letters of marque," which would permit merchant ships to go after English cargoes in piratical fashion, Congress enlarged the number of fighting ships quickly. The most successful privateer vessel was the *Dash*, out of Freeport.

A couple of Portland merchants who greatly admired prosperity had the *Dash* built at Porter's Landing in Freeport, and while subterfuge and finagling were rampant, nobody ever doubted that she was built for privateering. She had sixteen guns and accommodations for sixty seamen. When launched, she was rigged as a topsail schooner, but after trials she showed she could carry more sail, so she was rerigged as a morphadite brig with a ringtail. The ringtail was a sail bent on a spar off the main boom, and on the *Dash* it increased the size of the mainsail by one third. Nothing could catch and nothing could get away from the *Dash*. She was never outsailed, never struck by enemy fire, and never lost a "prize" she once set upon.

In seven cruises she took fifteen prizes, thus helping to win the war and to pay good wages to her crew and good earnings to her owners. Nobody knows, but probably her spread of sail was her own undoing. She disappeared, and conjecture was that an unexpected squall caught her with her ringtail peeled and she capsized— probably on George's Bank. All hands went down. Poet Whittier celebrated her in his "Dead Ship of Harpswell," a phantom vessel usually seen in a thick-o'-fog. The *Dash*, in fact, was no more than a warship, meant to capture enemy shipping at an agreed price, her "piracy" made honorable by the exigencies of war.

There is an instance of inland privateering that adds a little spice to Maine's activities during that war. In those days of friction with onetime Mother England, not all Mainers embraced the cause. In the revolution

such were "loyalists," but now they were sympathizers.
The War of 1812 did much harm to Maine business,
and pocketbooks are always sensitive. So there was a
sympathizer by the name of Moses Thompson, 1768 to
1831, who had gone up the Kennebec River as a young
man to take up some land in what is now the township
of Embden. By the time the war struck, he was well
situated. He had a thousand acres of fine meadowland
and timber, and his big "yellow house" was not only his
home and office, but an ordinary and tavern. It sat over-
looking the river, right by a ferry that soon gave way to
an iron bridge—across to Solon.

Uncle Moses was now the landed gentleman of the
settlement, respected for his prosperity and wisdom, and
something of a patron to those who came into the upper-
Kennebec valley to live. His yellow house was assessed
at $500, and he kept $300 at interest! Some neighbor
said one time that he and Uncle Mose owned more cattle than any other two men in the valley. It was so; the
neighbor had a cow and Uncle Mose owned the others.

By the year 1800 Uncle Mose had built up a considerable business in cattle—milch cows, beef animals, and
oxen. Periodically he would start a herd up the river
over a bushed-out trail into Canada, where he had a
ready market in the Chaudière River valley and at Quebec City. If anybody thinks cattle driving began with
the old Chisholm Trail to Abilene, let him think again.
The drives of Uncle Moses were not made over western
plains, but amounted instead to leisurely trips through
the forest, without remudas and chuck wagons. Cattle,
like hens, have their pecking order, and once a herd
settles on a leader, all you need do is show the leader
the way. The others follow. A man on ahead with a
firkin of grain keeps adroitly ahead of the leader, and
off they go. The two or three men needed to take a herd

into Canada were called drivers—Mainers didn't use the word "drover."

At the time the War of 1812 was peaking and Maine coastal folks were off doing their privateering, Uncle Moses got a herd together and started it upriver. He not only had his own fat and heavy animals from his own lush and well-kept acres, but he had cattle from neighbors on consignment, and others he'd bought up and down the valley. A man with a firkin on his arm led the way, and three or four men with knapsacks with supplies came on behind. Sort of a camping trip with a profit motive.

We'll never know who thought up and carried out the privateering attack on Uncle Moses's stately procession. That cattle drive never reached Canada. Instead, it was intercepted in the name of the United States of America and delivered down to the seacoast by a devious route. It was accepted by the proper government officials, and the usual percentage was awarded for the "prize."

Yes—there were those who believed Uncle Moses had been "in cahoots," and may have thought the thing up. Others felt his hired hands, his drivers, did him a snedricks. Then, there was the chance somebody from downstate played a part. We'll never know, will we? Uncle Moses was a known sympathizer, as he would be dealing in Canada, and after he got privateered he was even more so. He decried a government that would encourage piracy and reward the pirates at the expense of a solid citizen with money at interest and a public house where all were welcome and could find food and spirits of the finest kind at affordable prices. Things, he said, were at a pretty pass, and there were those who felt he had a point.

26

How the second coming of Jesus Christ was postponed in the town of Poland by the activities of the Ricker family, telling something about the miraculous efficacies of the gushing water of Poland Spring.

Maine's modest town of Poland is famous for its spring water, but it could just as well have been more famous for the Second Coming of Christ. Up to a late hour there is no further word on this miracle; reference is to the Shakers. The Shakers appeared on the religious scene in England about 1750, but the members of this odd sect preferred the name, "The United Society of Believers in Christ's Second Appearing." James Wardley and his wife Jane ticked the society off by withdrawing from the Quakers, or Friends. The Quakers merely trembled when spiritually aroused, but the new Shakers shook

and shivered and carried on and displayed their emotions in a more agitated manner. This distinction was
important at first, but in after years the Quakers didn't
quake so much and the Shakers didn't shake so much.
But Jane Wardley shook in a concentrated and abandoned way and claimed to have had "a call" and saw
visions. Her convulsive and palpitating piety was con-
vincing, and shortly the Shakers had many members.

In 1774 the mysteries of the Society were introduced
to America by Ann Lee, who settled in New York at
Mount Lebanon and claimed she was the New Christ
in His second time around. Soon thereafter several
Shakers settled in our town of Poland, which was then
known as Bakerstown. The Shakers were communistic
and celibate, good farmers and artisans, but because they
didn't breed new members were doomed to eventual
extinction. Adoptions helped, but new members from
the general public seldom appeared because of the stoic
and abstemious life in a Shaker colony. The Shakers
did many things well, but replenishing the earth was
not their strong point.

In 1794 the Shakers in Poland sold a part of their land
to one Jabez Ricker, a newcomer from Massachusetts.
His wife was Mary Wentworth of the prominent Wentworth family, and she and Jabez had been looking for
promising land that would support their ten children
and make a good home. Jabez made a wise move, but
the Shakers made a big mistake, as we shall see.

The land Jabez bought is now known as Ricker Hill.
On the morning after he took possession, a knock came
to the door of Jabez's cabin, and when he opened, two
wayfarers were there to ask for breakfast. They said
they had just been refused food down the road, because
the Shakers didn't fancy feeding "people of the world."

This was another mistake, because Jabez now realized he was on a traveled route, and that he was willy-nilly an innkeeper. He fed the two men, and that was the beginning of the Poland Spring Hotel.

Right away Jabez began building a house, and from the first nail he meant to have a place that would take in travelers and feed them. His house thus became the Mansion House, and was the starting point for the vast complex that would one day occupy the whole hill and be renowned the world around. The water from the boiling spring on Ricker HIll would bring on fame and fortune, but Jabez was long gone before the water became famous.

Jabez kept adding to the Mansion House, and in 1834 the property passed to his son Wentworth. Wentworth died in 1837, and in turn his son took over—Hiram. Hiram, at twenty-five, had been working in a clothing store in Boston and was considered prosperous, so he debated with himself about going back into Maine to run a farm and take transients. His decision to return to Maine came easily, however, since he had "dyspepsia." Another name at the time was "humor of the stomach," which meant Hiram was uncomfortable all the time, his food didn't agree with him, and he was touchy and grouchy. Maine air would, he thought, do him a lot of good, so he gave his notice and went back to Ricker Hill.

The Mansion House was by now attracting seasonal guests, and life on the farm was geared to giving them every comfort and pleasure. The bubbling spring by the pasture gate was used, but nobody had yet placed any commercial value on it. Hiram, in his dyspeptic discomfort, stumbled on the magnificent asset. While helping get in the hay in July of 1884, Hiram took a thirst and walked over to the spring for a drink. He quaffed, and at once realized that his gastric disturbance was relieved; within minutes he was freed of the nagging he had endured for years. He took another drink, and shortly realized the water had acted as a cathartic, immediate and compelling. It reamed Hiram out in good shape, and he never again was troubled with his humor of the stomach. He lived for years in eupeptic bliss, and frequently attributed his recovery to the "medicinal" virtues of the Poland Spring water.

And every time Hiram spoke thus, somebody would recall another instance of the same. Grandfather Jabez, for instance, had always filled up on this spring water when he removed his winter underwear in the spring, and besides a fine cleansing of the bowels, he came forth a new man, ready for the summer. Jabez always said the spring had a special quality. Then somebody recalled that Father Wentworth had been cured of kidney gravel by drinking the water. Nobody thought much about it at the time, but he did take a full pitcher of that spring water with every meal. The recollection about Wentworth's kidney stones caused Dr. Elephalet Clark, who was curious, to put some kidney stones in a bottle of Poland Spring water, and they dissolved! Then a man offered his testimonial that not only had he been cured of his kidney disorder, but the water also cured his ox! The ox had been driven to the pasture in its extremity and left to die, but water from the Ricker Spring had revived it. During that summer the ox gained six inches in girth and fattened, and come fall was sold for prime beef at a profit.

This needs to be said: The water from this Poland Spring is not unlike water from many another boiling spring in that part of Maine. It flows underground from the eastern slope of the White Mountains, and bubbles forth with artesian pressure. None of these many springs can be called "medicinal," but in 1859 the imputation had a salutary value for the Ricker hotel business. One woman who had "incurable constipation" drank a three-quart pail of the Poland Spring water and was completely cured. She lived forty years after that in serene regularity. Such proof could not be ignored. It was in 1859 that Hiram Ricker sold his first three-gallon demijohn of Poland Spring water for fifteen cents. In two years he was selling one thousand barrels, and from then on things flowed right along. In a few years the claim of medicinal properties was eased off, and the pitch became merely its purity and that it was good for you.

The Mansion House and the new Poland Spring House became a tremendous property—and the spring water was the big booster. For the guests, the place spared no luxury. Guests arrived by Pullman at Danville Junction and were trotted the five miles to Ricker Hill in Concord coaches and tallyhos behind four and six teams, and upon approaching the hotel they paused by the spring house where glasses of pure Poland Water were passed up by attendants. Then on to the hotel and fun! Poland Water served at table was never chilled; fresh from the spring it was cool, and ice would taint it. Guest after guest over the years asked the same question—did the hotel use Poland Water in the plumbing? (No, it did not; lake water was pumped for all but drinking.) The golf "links" was laid out. Members of the Boston Symphony Orchestra played daily concerts. Lectures, art exhibits, nature walks—nothing was neglected. Food? Finest in the world. Name your heart's desire, and there it was!

And always pure Poland Water fresh from that

remarkable bubbling spring to refresh you and, if you needed it, to cure you. In 1918 when shortages gave other resorts some problems, guests at Poland Spring hardly knew there was a war going on. The Rickers tilled 500 acres, with 125 of them in table vegetables. Five acres of green peas, seven acres of green beans, 3,000 tomato plants, 500 hills of cucumbers—then sweet corn, beets, carrots . . . They kept 100 head of milking cows.

Poland Spring water is still on sale, although the big Ricker hotel business finished its day. You can't find a better water. And you can get it almost anywhere in the world. But the day of the fine resort hotel ended when the automobile made everybody an "overnight guest." True Poland Spring guests came for the week, the month, the season. Efforts to keep the place going were gallant, but an era had ended. One night, long after the last of the Rickers, the big Poland Spring House burned flat. It lapsed into loving memory along with a good many other resort hotels that had already given up the struggle—the Rangeley Lake House, the Belgrade Lake House, Squaw Mountain Inn, the Samoset, Mount Kineo Hotel, and even the Summit House right across the valley in Poland. The Summit House was for people who couldn't get in at Poland Spring—the Rickers were not open-minded in some ways.

"Ayeh—now that you ask . . . You want a good Poland Spring story, eh? Well, you've come to the right party, for I've lived here under Ricker Hill all my life—so far. Let me see—how about this fellow named Judson, or Hubbard, or some such thing, and he came up here from down Boston way to try the water? He had see-roses of the liver bad. Been aggervatin' him for years. Been to every doc and clinic, even to specialists in

Europe, and not a thing anybody could do for him. He had it some old bad, he did. Well, he'd tried Saratoga, and he'd tried all them other waters, and he knew that Poland Spring was going to be his last resort. Old Hiram was alive then, and he took one look at this Hudson, or Judson, or whatever, and he knew right off the man is beyond help. Peak-id and run down, all yaller in the face, and his hands twitching like a musician who's dreaming he's playing a harp. Anyway, Hiram took the man in and settled him in a ten-dollar room, and they began pushing the Poland Water to him. Quart or two at a time, and always somebody coming with another pitcher. Regular parade of waitresses and busboys, and they rasped this fellow out for fair in no time at all.

"Well, he perked up some and said he felt better. After a week he was eating like a horse and had his color back and he didn't twitch. Before the end of July he was playing golf and going swimming and hiking on the bird tours. You'd swear he never had a sick day in his life. His liver complaint was cured and he was a new man. He went home to Boston and had a case of Poland Water shipped to him every week. Never drank anything else as long as he lived. And he lived another fifty years. That's the best Poland Water story I know, and I guess one time or another I've heard 'em all.

"Well, come to think of it, there's one more thing. When that fellow died, he was in such good health that before they could sign a death certificate, the coroner had to take the man's liver out in the dooryard and kill it with a club."

Isn't it stimulating to wonder how the Shakers would be doing today if they hadn't sold to Jabez Ricker?

27

A few reasonable thoughts as to why certain Maine towns are named Poland, Moscow, Athens, Denmark, etc., when nobody from there was here; and then the perfectly understandable explanation of Norway.

In the considerable list of Maine towns that took their names from foreign places, the only ones that make sense are New Sweden and Stockholm. Not Sweden, which has no connection with Sweden, but *New* Sweden, which is far up in Aroostook County and, like Stockholm next to it, was settled in 1870 by true Swedes from Sweden. Plain Sweden is next to Bridgton, downstate. Otherwise, such place-names in Maine seem to have derived strictly from whimsy. There were no Portuguese in Lisbon; Austrians in Vienna; French in Calais; Russians in Moscow; Danes in Denmark; Greeks in Athens;

and certainly no bums in Gilead. It's possible seafaring had something to do with this—Mainers knew about foreign places, and many of them had been there. Moreover, the foreign names were adjusted immediately to Maine ways; Vienna became vigh-enny, Madrid is ma-a-a-a-drid, Bremen is bree-m'n, Peru is a straightforward proo, Calais is reasonably cal-l's, and Gilead is gil-y'd. Lisbon seems to have derived sensibly; the folks there thought Thompsonborough was too long to write on a postal card, so they simplified. The real crazy explanation belongs to Norway. It wasn't supposed to be Norway at all.

Not a little of Norway's stature comes from some sixty veterans of the American Revolution who took up land grants there as their war bonuses. Not too many of them were Mainers; most were veterans of Massachusetts militia companies, but Maine was part of the Bay State then, and the General Court of Massachusetts had charge of such grants. Contrary to most schoolbook piffle, these revolutionary soldiers were not yokels and rustics and bumpkins who got excited one day and grabbed up pitchforks and handscythes and came running to quell the dirty Redcoats. They were, instead, veterans of weekly musterings in trainbands—every colonial village had a muster ground. The "minutemen" were capable soldiers with good equipment, quite ready to take on the King's regulars. The officers were not babboons and makeshifts, but knew their tactics well, and were as proficient as anything the English fielded. Which means that our town of Norway had the early advantage of a solid group of citizens well schooled in the rudiments of Americanism—not the kind to take something they didn't like lying down. It's hard to believe they allowed their town to be called Norway.

Well, one of the revolutionary veterans in Norway was Sam Ames, who had popped up here and there during the war and had a flair for being at the right place at the right time. He was the drummer at the surrender of Burgoyne's army at Saratoga, and not many Maine towns will beat that! After he got settled in Norway he would break out his drum at the slightest invitation, and retell about "Gentleman Johnny" Burgoyne's graceful capitulation, done with all the social charms and polite gestures, something like a quadrille.

Another veteran was Lem Shield, who had been assigned as orderly to General Washington, but always explained that he was really the bodyguard. If it hadn't been for Lem Shield . . .

Then there as Jake Frost, an unlucky youngster who got a British musketball in the hip at Bunker Hill. It walloped him and knocked him twenty feet, effectively removing him from the fray. He lay there in pain and watched the English go up, and then come down, and then go up again, and finally they didn't come down right away. The English gave him field attention and then sent him to Halifax as a prisoner of war. He and some others dug an escape tunnel, but Jake was sore and lame from his wound and he couldn't travel well. One day he was hiding until dark under a fallen tree, and the guards sent out to find him came and sat on the tree while they ate their lunch and talked things over. Jake listened very quietly, and after dark he hobbled along towards home. He died in Norway in 1839, and two-three years before he died a doctor removed the musketball—Jake had lugged it around for fifty years.

And there was Phineas Whitney, another veteran of Bunker Hill. He had fired point-blank during the first two charges of the British, and was loaded and ready for the next charge. But by now the militia knew the jig was up—they were out of powder, and it would be hand-to-hand on the next assault. When the English came up the hill again, the officer in charge was urging them on, and just as the Redcoats reached the redoubt the officer shouted something like "This time we'll make it!" and just then Phineas Whitney shot him. That was the end of Major John Pitcairn.

Major John Pitcairn? He was the one who ordered eight hundred British Redcoats to fire on seventy militiamen at Lexington on April 19, 1775, the first skirmish of the American Revolution. On that day, after that volley, the militiamen (all but eight of them) retired—to regroup and to be joined by other minutemen for the next encounter at Concord. But at Bunker Hill, the retirement of Phineas Whitney after he shot Major John Pitcairn was much more precipitous. His discharged musket, now no good to him, was discarded, and off he took as fast as he could trot in the general direction of Worcester. True, the British gained the day, but the stand the militiamen had made gave courage to the colonists, and showed that the British regulars weren't such a much.

Well, the misnaming of Norway was a clerical blunder. An early proprietor had been named Rust, and after him the settlement became Rustfield. It's true the name Norway appears in at least a dozen other places in Maine, without context with the present town of Norway, and quite likely without reference to Norway in Europe. Nobody in Rustfield had the slightest intention of naming the place Norway. The name they put on the petition for incorporation was Norage, and one guess is as good as another. Some have fancied it was an attempt at Norwich, which in those days our forefathers would have pronounced "norridge," but there was nobody in Rustfield connected with Norwich, a borough in England. "Norridge" amounted to an Indian word for waterfalls, but how it should be spelled is up for grabs. Father Sebastian Rasle had produced a dictionary of the Abnaki tongue in his time, reducing whatever an Indian said to French, and such was the early relationship of Indians and Frenchman that we Englishers know only what a word spoken in Indian sounded like to a Frenchman. Norridge? It's the word seen in Norridgewock, but to the folks of Rustfield it seemingly came out as Norage, and that's what they wanted to be called.

But some foolish clerk in the legislative offices in Boston, one of these editorial whizzbangs who have much knowledge and small sense, saw "Norage" as clearly a mistake ("Those jokers up in Mayne can't spell, you know!"), and he crossed out Norage and wrote in Norway. The incorporation bill was passed, and Norway it was and Norway it is.

At this late date, maybe we should wonder why Phineas Whitney didn't go to Boston and take care of that clerk.

28

Various abstractions also made good names for Maine towns; and when it comes to Friendship, we have an account of a voyage that shows how the Down-East sea captains traded in foreign ports.

The dozen or so Maine towns named for abstractions occasion inquiry from tourists, and one answer is that the settlers felt that way and thought the names were good ones. Unity, as an example, was so named because of local "unison in political sentiment," although today Unity rolls show 314 Republicans and 141 Democrats. So, mostly, Friendship was friendly, Liberty and Freedom admired liberty and freedom, and in Amity peace and good fellowship prevailed. Just why the wildland township of Misery, up in Somerset County, was so named is easy—it's the way people in Misery would feel if anybody had lived there at the time.

A happy difference prevails with Hope. It would be

nice to know that somebody settling in that blueberry and Christmas tree township had hope about something, but one story tells us the name is a complete and bland happenstance. Jim Malcolm, hired to survey the proposed township (Hope was incorporated in 1804), went about setting up his stone posts and wooden stakes, and for witness points he daubed letters on them with a paintbrush. Somebody noticed that the four cornerstones of the town were marked O, P, E, and H. Back up one stone and take that again.

Harmony was a wildland grant to Hallowell Academy, after the colonial custom of subsidizing education, and Charles Vaughn bought it from the academy trustees. The idea that funds from such a sale would keep the academy in clover forever seems to have evaporated over the years. Charles Vaughn followed the usual plan in developing the place. He sold off lots, keeping certain advantages for himself, and served well as the "proprietor." The place was accordingly called Vaughnstown until it came time to incorporate it as the 141st town in 1803. Now the several inhabitants felt it would be pleasant to name the new community Harmony "to perpetuate the life of harmony as it existed in the town among the inhabitants." Splendid idea! It seems, however, that some dissonance arose over this, and the harmonious nature of the inhabitants stood at recess until agreement could be restored. Harmony almost lost to those who felt Vaughnstown was good enough.

Union and Unity are two separate towns—and it is said that the biblical observation that it is fitting for brethren to dwell together in unity was once exemplified by two brothers there who had their pictures in the Bangor *Commercial*. Union also drew its name from the harmony that prevailed, and when incorporated in 1786 it had seventy-seven residents. But it had already gone through two previous designations—Taylortown and Sterlington.

The town of Industry suggests high optimism. Anybody who settled there needed a lot of it, and the idea of farming those ledges suggests despair. 'Tis said that Industry has great wealth in good glacial gravel, except that none of it is smaller than a bushel basket.

Not usually included in the list of Maine abstractions is The Enchanted. Perhaps the two townships with this name—Upper Enchanted and Lower Enchanted—are neglected because they're tucked out of the way and not well known. They're in somerset County and entirely wild and unincorporated land. In the original surveys they were 2R5 and 3R6 in Bingham's Kennebec Purchase, west of the Kennebec River. Nobody knows what whimsy prompted the fairyland name, but it includes an Enchanted Pond, from which flows Enchanted Stream. Eventually Enchanted Stream flows into the Dead river, which is the West Branch of the Kennebec River after the split at The Forks. Now you know where you are.

Technology was once a post office in East Machias, but was discontinued because of the nuisance of being confused with MIT. How about Strong? Years ago somebody tried to start a story that Strong was named for the great strength of a legendary Indian who lived there—one Pierpole. He could make Hercules look like a puny weakling. Then some said it wasn't his strength, but the way he smelled. Before this could be settled, Pierpole left Strong and went up into Canada to join the St. Francis tribe. Actually, Strong was named for Governor Caleb Strong of Massachusetts, 1800 to 1807. In 1801 he signed the incorporation papers of the town of Strong—the first such papers of his incumbency.

A part of the town of Hollis is called Moderation.

And next to Misery township is the township of Misery Gore—a gore is an irregular plot of land where survey-ors' lines diverge, usually in error. Maine had numerous gores, indicating numerous errors, but most of them have been absorbed by adjacent townships. Prout's Gore lies in Freeport. But Coburn Gore is still a full township, on the Canadian boundry in Franklin County, and its previous designation was Twp. 3, Range 7, west of Bingham's Kennebec Purchase—which means fidelity.

Friendship seems to have the best stories. True, some say the name derives from the amicable nature of Friendshippers, but another version is that a vessel came into the harbor back around 1800, when the folks of Meduncook were thinking of incorporating, which they did in 1807. Meduncook was Indian, and still applies to coastal waters adjacent to Friendship. An Indian who had been given a handout by an early housewife fin-ished his meal and passed her the plate with the remark "Me done, cook!" This absurdity didn't appeal to the folks, so they began trying to think of a good name. That's when this vessel came in from the ocean and tied up. Friendship's (or Meduncook's) harbor enticed ves-sels passing the Monhegan area, both as a good place to pause and as a place to trade. A couple of Meduncook-ers standing on the wharf saw the vessel's name on the transom—FRIENDSHIP.

"Sakes-a-mighty, Sol," says Tom, "why ain't that a fit name for our town?"

"Finest kind," said Sol, and the idea caught on.

There were several vessels named *Friendship* in the general area at the time; any of them could have put in at Meduncook. One, in particular, had a voyage of suf-ficient frustrations to get her into the books. She put out of Wells with a cargo of lumber, headed for St. Vincent in the Windwards, Captain Theodore Wells in command. Her cargo was hewn Maine lumber, and the owners had instructed Captain Wells not to dispose of it unless he could get a hundred gallons of molasses for every thousand board feet of lumber.

The schooner had a quick and uneventful passage to St. Vincent, but Captain Wells arrived to find the market depressed. So he headed for Grenada, but that was "no sale," too. He went to Trinidad, to Port Royal at Martinico, to Bastarre at Guadeloupe. Then to Nevis. At Nevis he got an offer that enticed him, but felt the buyers of doubtful solvency, so he pushed on to St. Thomas. At St. Thomas there was no demand whatever for hewn timber, so he was down to his last chance— Puerto Rico was the last island that had molasses, except Cuba, but he was doubtful about lumber in Cuba. On his way to Puerto Rico a fresh blow and thick weather drove the schooner *Friendship* right on past. So he adjusted and went to St. Domingo, but found the market dull and no sale.

Captain Wells kept on to Aux Cayes, to Jérémie, to Mariguana, and to Port-au-Prince. Here he found several vessels making losing sales in a glutted market. So he went to St. Marks. After all this jigging and jogging, he went back to Jérémie, where he spent twenty-eight more days dickering before he sold. Then Captain Wells waited forty days for a cargo of coffee—close enough to his owners' orders so he knew they'd be happy. Coffee was good cargo. He sailed for home.

He made it, but the *Friendship* and the coffee didn't. The vessel went down just a few days out of Jérémie. Perhaps—perhaps!—to be immortalized in the name of Maine's most friendly town.

29

The story of Alvin Orland Lombard and his ingenious contribution to the progress of human locomotion and mechanical achievement, with the sad news of the demise of an innocent man, Roary MacLaren.

The wheel was not invented in the State of Maine. A turning point, so to speak, in the progress of civilization, the wheel was invented in prehistoric times in Southeast Asia, probably by a Southeast Asian. But nobody in thousands of years really improved on the wheel until 1900, when Alvin Orland Lombard of Waterville, Maine, made his first steam log hauler. Instead of wheels, as on a railroad locomotive, his log hauler had cleated lugs—the first "caterpillar" traction. Logs in the Maine woods were handled in winter on snow, so wheels were not much use. Alvin's improvement on the wheel was described simply as a "logging engine," and he was issued patent number 674,737 for it on May 4, 1901. It, too, was a turning point in the progress of civilization.

Alvin Lombard had a machine shop, and as a mill-wright had gone to Millinocket when the Great Northern Paper Company was organized. There was much talk within the industry at that time about the need for a mechanical log hauler that would supersede the oxen and horses. In the beginnings of Maine lumbering, logs were harvested close to the sawmills and hauling was not too much of a problem. Even as the cuttings moved inland, hauling logs was limited to the distance to a river, and the annual spring drives floated the logs the rest of the way to mill. But by 1900 lumbercamps were deeper in the back country, too far for oxen and horses, and the single sled load of logs a pair of animals could bring out ran the costs too high.

The machinists and millwrights working for GNPCo talked about this, and agreed there was a need for some kind of engine that would run on snow, not on tracks like a railroad locomotive, and would be able to pull a considerable train of logging sleds. One of the mach-insts was Johnson Woodbury of Patten, who had already made shop drawings of his version of caterpillar trac-tion, but Woodbury never went beyond the drawings. Lombard had already perfected and patented a pulp-wood barker and a turbine governor, indicating that he thought ahead, and back in his Waterville shop he soon had his own drawings of cleated-track power and was designing a log hauler.

His was not the first attempt. Joe Peavey, the Still-water blacksmith who gave lumbering the hand tool called a peavey, already had a log hauler working, except that it didn't work. Everybody came to look at it, and expected great things. The traction came from two huge screws that were meant to work the machine along as they turned. As the thread on a carpenter's woodscrew draws into the wood, so these screws went along the ground. Peavey's engine worked fine on solid ground, although its speed didn't set any records, but when it got onto snow or soft earth it dug itself in and sat there in quiet desuetude. Peavey never made his second log hauler.

Lombard's first steam log hauler had an upright boiler, but later he laid the boiler horizontal, so the machine looked more like a railroad engine—except for the lugs and except for the steering mechanism up front. Lacking rails to guide it, his engine needed a helmsman. Where a railroad locomotive has forward pony wheels, the Lombard had a sled. It served as a front-end rudder.

But the Lombard operated on snow, and in all, Alvin made eighty-three of the things before heavy trucks and good timberland roads took over. As fast as his shop could turn them out, the lumber companies built "log hauls" for them, and soon in every part of the state lumber came out of the woods by sled train, with the Lombard clanking and churning and chuffing and doing what it was made to do. Since Alvin Lombard had his mind focused on log hauling, he neglected other aspects of his property. One day he heard that two companies in California were making farm machinery that infringed on his patent. He sued and got a judgment, but judgments don't always mean recovery, and Lombard never got a penny. Worse luck, one of those California companies had registered a copyright for the name "caterpillar," and that was that.

Much of the Lombard log hauler was made of cast

iron, and the quality was poor. In very cold weather the cast iron might crack with frost. Lombards needed constant care and attention, and even so they would burst and blow up and break down. So the Lombard company in Waterville did a big business in repair parts, and was prosperous.

But there were accidents. Roary MacLaren from Prince Edward Island hired out as a chopper, and started to walk into camp at Masardis when a Lombard came by with a train of sleds, banging and bumping and belching smoke and sparks into the cold winter sky. Roary had never seen a log hauler, so he set down his packsack and watched, entranced. Amazing! Up front, riding "headlight," was the steersman, guiding the great monster down the graded log haul towards the waiting mill. Up in the cab was the engineer; when he saw Roary standing there he tootled the whistle at him. Roary waved. And just then something on the Lombard exploded, and a fragment of cast iron caught Roary on his forehead and killed him on the spot.

The next month a letter came to the Lombard Steam Log Hauler Company in Waterville. It was written from Prince Edward Island by a Jamie MacLeod, who wanted to place an order. MacLeod said they didn't have a thing on Prince Edward Island that could kill a MacLaren, and he wanted to buy two Lombards.

The two tractor makers in California who "stole" Lombard's idea were, however, pikers—as it turned out. On September 15, 1916, the British army moved against German positions in the Battle of the Somme. The appearance of the first "tank" was a complete surprise to the Germans, and once again there was a turning point in man's progress. The "tank" was equipped with Lombard log hauler cleated traction—a device a soldier described in his letter home as "a track that lays itself down and then picks itself up again." But again, Alvin Lombard collected not one penny for infringements. The word "tank," as applied to a fighting machine, was used by the English while they were producing their battle wagons to keep the nature of the thing secret. Nobody supposed a "tank" would turn out to be a tank. Nobody in Maine thought a Lombard would, either.

An overworked Maine pleasantry has to do with icing the log hauls. The log hauls were roadways, laid out in the summer with tree trunks laid crosswise—corduroy. Dirt was added where needed. When snow fell and the winter timber harvest could begin, everything was packed down for smoothness, and an icing crew would begin applying water to the surface. Every night the water cart, which was a tank mounted on sled runners, would pass along the log haul dripping water that froze immediately. When the Lombard went to work at daybreak, the log haul was newly slick. Icing was not at all a pleasant job, and the men who did it would come in for breakfast encased in ice like knights of the Table Round in fighting armor.

So the pleasantry was about a traveling salesman who was making his first trip into Maine and took a room for the night in the Huston House at Mattawamkeag. As the temperature dropped to $-40°$ F. along about midnight, this salesman found himself cold in bed, and seeking some more blankets he descended to the hotel lobby. There, the big pot belly stove glowed, and it appealed to this salesman. So he pulled up a chair, and instead of going back to bed he sat there in comfort—blankets wrapped about him, toasty warm.

Just before daybreak Henry Baker, who had been working all night on an icing crew, came into the lobby clinking and glistening from the ice sheet that had formed. The salesman looked up as he heard the door close behind Henry, and in utter disbelief of what he saw he said, "My God, man! What room do you have?"

Besides restored Lombard log haulers (there's one at the Lumberman's Museum at Patten), the machines live on in a Maine metaphor. Not too often, but now and then you will hear somebody described as being "a regular Lombard of a man!" That's a lum-b'd, as Mainers say it. It means he's big, powerful, able—a man to do his day's work and more. One who doesn't tire and give up. Two ax handles between his shoulder blades. And not always with finesse—the Lombard clanked and churned, and a man who is like a regular Lombard may be a bit gormy and sometimes apply brute strength when he might do the work easier if he'd stop and think a little. He gets the job done, but with a good deal of rammin' 'round.

Next time you see anything with caterpillar traction, you can tell people they stole that from Alvin Lombard of Waterville, Maine.

30

Frank Farrar, well worthy of the honor, appears in this historical work a second time, now as the guiding hand for the Ancient & Honorable Sabattus Valley Fox & Hound Club, long a Maine institution.

Harvesting ice, a business lost in a forgotten past, once gave Maine its best export product and its most profitable venture. The year Maine was separated from Massachusetts, 1820, Captain Bill Bradstreet came up the Kennebec river late in the fall and lingered at a Gardiner wharf into early winter. His brig *Orion*, frozen in, became his prison for the winter. Gardiner is the Maine city where first prize is a week and second prize is two weeks, so we should sympathize with the captain and lament his poor judgment that kept him from sailing before ice formed. But all was not lost. Come spring, the ice broke up, and Captain Bill yanked enough of it aboard to fill the *Orion*'s hold. Then he drifted down on the next tide and high-tailed for Baltimore, where he sold his cargo to fish packers and made $700 profit. Since the ice cost him nothing, he liked that fine, and he went into the ice business.

Before long, harvesting and shipping ice gave Maine a new fame all over the world. There had been ice cutting on the Hudson River, but the seasons were up and down, and the Kennebec River could be counted on. In a new day it's hard to picture the activity on the Kennebec every January, with thousands of men working to fill the vast icehouses. After ice-out, vessels came to transport cakes of ice to southerly cities, and even to the Orient. Sawdust, free for the scooping, insulated the ice in holds so a vessel could reach even Calcutta with a sound cargo.

Along about 1860 one Jim Cheeseman brought ice harvesting into major proportions. A warm winter south of Boston made Kennebec ice, fifteen inches thick, look attractive, and Cheeseman laid up some thirty thousand tons. The next year he did better. And he found no fault with the Civil War, when Uncle Sam began paying well for ice to preserve army foods. Jim was in comfortable circumstances. Furthermore, wartime need for ice promoted peacetime use, and the city folks were interested in cool drinks and ice cream. The "ice chest" proliferated, and would remain until some nut invented the mechanical refrigerator. In 1880 Maine cut and shipped three million tons of ice. But by 1900 consolidation of harvesting and distributing wrought changes that tapered Maine's ice business off. Charles W. Morse of Bath merged the ice companies supplying Boston, New York, Washington, Philadelphia, and Baltimore, and after that ice was harvested mostly on the Hudson again.

An aspect of the Maine ice harvest thus far ignored was the impact of thousands of tramps, bums, hoboes, vagrants, and sundry seasonal visitors who began arriving along about Christmas to assist in the harvest. The ice in the Kennebec River would be covered with men during the harvest—clearing away snow, grooving for the cakes, working ice toward the chutes that led into the huge icehouses. Tiering the cakes for storage and covering them with hay and sawdust kept more men at work inside. At the peak of Maine ice cutting, twenty-five thousand men worked at it. Until steam machinery was developed, at least a thousand horses were used. True, Maine farmers and woodsmen worked on the ice, but the first of our country's "migrant workers" made a horde of seasonal visitors that had considerable effect on Maine ways.

For one thing, it conditioned the Maine housewife to the "handout." "Tramp" was the customary word; there was no hitchhiking then and unless a man rode the dangerous brakerods of a freight train, he walked. A woman making her family's breakfast could look up and see a tramp in the lane, and she'd reach for an extra plate. Usually, but not always, the tramp would be asked to do some small chore to pay for his handout—split a little wood, sweep out the shop, whatever. Many a farm had a "tramp room," a place in a shed where a wanderer could sleep. Some tramps got to be known by name. One such was Shadrack, who was good at sharpening tools. After ice cutting Shadrack would wander about, and the woman would greet him, "Good morning, Shadrack," and hand him her kitchen knives and a whetstone. Most tramps who came for handouts would know where the bucksaw hung, and would work at the woodpile before going to rap on the door.

Forgotten is that kind of Maine tramp, and forgotten also is the Ancient & Honorable Sabattus Valley Fox & Hound Club. This sporting society was the development of Frank Farrar soon after he returned from the Civil War. Frank had his father's butcher shop and made an effort to have a meat market. He kept a hog hanging up in his cool box (which used pond ice) but sometimes was "fresh out." Frank had numerous other interests, and he had his soldier's pension, so his butcher shop gradually became a kind of cultural institution where friends gathered to cheer each other and meditate on many things. There were fastidious ladies who lamented that such goings-on were permitted in a decent community, but truth to tell the Sabattus Valley Fox & Hound Club remained fairly esoteric and didn't create undue disturbances. Besides the intellectual discussions, the members conducted seminars on cribbage and high-low-jack and made no public appearances other than the occasional fox hunt. These were, it must be admitted, notable, but were always conducted with a dignity nobody could honestly fault.

On the morning selected for a fox hunt, Luther Butt would bring around his pair of high-stepping horses, attached to the express wagon owned by the Fox Club, and he would anchor them in front of the Farrar Market with a hitching weight. One of these fox hunts was not at all like the traditional British yoicks-away excursion, red jackets and plug hats, clavichords and bugles, and tallyho. Frank's friends, members all, were never tipplers, but were collectively aware of the efficacy of October cider when exposed to positive thinking into, say, February. They knew, too, that a lacing with

Caldwell's Newburyport Rum imparted a flavor completely unknown to teetotalers. Then, for the picnic, each member brought food. The members, now assembled, would stow their effects in the wagon and set out for the picnic grounds already selected for this outing.

The club had numerous such grounds, all of them at a "crossing." When hounds start a fox, the fox will run in circles, and the circle is dictated by the lay of the land. Sooner or later a fox would pass a road or a brook and that was a "crossing." Once the dogs were released, the members could go to a crossing and have lunch. However, many times the members of the Sabattus Valley Fox & Hound wouldn't shoot, but would cheer the fox as he passed and continue to drink lunch. Now and then the fox population would build up until farmers complained about stolen hens, and then the members would perform a public service and shoot.

This particular February morning was magnificent. The sun is getting higher in February, and some mornings pleasantly presage springtime. On such a morning the maple trees will begin to draw sap, and stray birds from the southland appear. Frank Farrar, who scheduled fox hunts, had picked a dandy. The Butt horses were ready, and the members were up in the wagon, sitting fore and aft on two settees with dogs and lunches between. Shotguns stood between knees. The club made an imposing sight. Frank Farrar put up his little sign that said "CLOSED FOR THE DURATION," and got up on the front seat with Luther, shotgun between his knees. Frank had two jugs of cider, one quart of Caldwell's Newburyport Rum, and a mince pie. That was for him; the others had their own. "Drive on!" said Frank.

Although some deplored this club, it did have a wait-

ing list. Membership was limited by the size of the
wagon, and today all were present; Reuben Mulhol-
land, Abner Whitehall, Chauncey (Jigger) Blake, Ruel
Peabody, Snick-snack (Forrest) Hobson, Levi Flanders,
and Dr. Bronson McFadden, the veterinarian and official keeper of the hounds. Luther clucked at his team,
and off went the fox club, headed for today's picnic at
the Kettlebottom crossing over in Webster. As the wagon
went out of sight, Dr. McFadden blew a pitchpipe and
the members began singing the club anthem:

> Down on the farm, they all ask for you—
> Down on the farm, they all ask for you—
> Down on the farm, they all ask for you—
> > The pigs ask,
> > > The cows ask,
> > > > The horses ask for you.

It was indeed a merry moment. Jig's redbone hound,
who would rather sing than run foxes, joined in. After
the anthem, the members sang "John Brown Knows My
Father, My Father Knows John Brown" to the tune of
"Onward Christian Soldiers," and shortly the wagon
was up on the Kingsbury Road and nearly halfway to
the Kettlebottom crossing.

And the club now came upon a farmhouse where a
gentleman was splitting wood by a considerable woodpile. As the wagon came abreast Frank Farrar spied a
handsome Brahma rooster close by the woodpile—a
magnificent spectacle. The Brahma rooster of good carriage with stand as much as seven or eight hands high,
with formidable brow, wattles like beanbags, tail of
sweep and billow, and feathers up and down his legs.
It suddenly entered Frank Farrar's fancy that this bird,

plucked and roasted properly, would add greatly to today's picnic, so he said to Luther, "Stop the horses!" Luther said, "Whoa!"

Frank spoke to the gentleman splitting wood.

"Good morning, kind friend," he said. "May I inquire into the state of your health?" Frank stood five feet two when he was standing, but he made up for that with graceful carriage and stately language. A stranger might fancy him a retired Presbyterian clergyman.

The gentleman laid his ax down on the chopping block, indicating a lull in his labors, and he said, "Nicely, thank you."

Frank said, "I admire that rooster. He'd make a fine dinner!"

"Yes," said the gentleman.

Frank said, "What would you charge for a shot at him?"

The gentleman looked over at the Brahma rooster and waggled his head as if pondering such an absurd proposition. Then he shrugged his shoulders and said, "Oh-h-h-h—fifty cents?" His rising inflection suggested he thought fifty cents might be a little high.

"Fifty cents?" said Frank. "Well, that's a deal. Just to show I'm a good sport, I'll make that seventy-five! Here you are, sir!" Frank tossed a half and a quarter, which the gentleman caught deftly and put in his pocket. He picked up the ax.

Frank stood up in the wagon and brought his shotgun to position. Luther held the reins should the horses take a fright at the noise. Frank said, "Gentlemen!" Then the members of the fox club stood up and brought their guns to position. "Fire!" said Frank.

The broadside set the wagon over in the road a good ten inches. Before Frank could descend to retrieve his bird, a woman appeared from the house with an anguished shriek of dismay, and in a voice that peeled bark from trees, she yelled, "You drunken fools, whatever have you done?" Frank, halfway to the ground, held his position while she went on.

"You've shot my rooster! Why, why, why! You've shot my prize Brahma rooster! You drunk, good-for-nothing idiots! You shot him! That bird took a blue and was best in show at State Fair, and you came by and shot him! You're all crazy drunk!"

"Madam," said Frank with composure and gentlemanly aplomb, "allow me to explain. You abuse us. We have merely completed a business arrangement and have done nothing to warrant your vilification and contumely. In good faith and with honest intentions, we paid as agreed, and we entered into a straightforward arrangement with your husband here. . . ."

"Husband?" she screamed. "Husband? You idiots—he's no husband. He's an ice tramp splitting wood for his breakfast!"

31

A not-too-interesting account of the first city and the largest town in North America, being Gorgeana and Madawaska, with an explanation of the place called Quack; a Canadian gets elected to Maine legislature.

Quack, Maine, might well have been the first city in America, but it wasn't. The first city in America was Gorgeana, and confusing Gorgeana with Quack was just a mistake. One Captain Levett made the mistake. He came sailing along the coast of Maine in 1623 looking for a place to settle, and like Henry David Thoreau on the East Branch, Levett didn't know where he was a good part of the time. When he came to the place we now call Portland he liked the looks of it, and as he had one of those grants the Plymouth Company handed out to settlers, he took up his claim to a place the Indians called Quack. Next he built a house on an island. It may be that he put his house on House Island, but he also claimed Cushing, Peak, and Diamond Islands, so it may be that he didn't. The house was long since gobbled up by the high taxes in Portland, so we don't know. After he finished his house he sailed back to England to fetch settlers, but he never returned to Maine.

Because he set down in his journal that he built a house at Quack, one of our agile Maine historians assumed that he meant York, just on the grounds of sound-alike. At the time of Levett, Maine didn't have any York, and the settlement where York was to come later was called Agamenticus. Out of this improbable confusion early York was now and then called Quack.

York is Maine's second oldest town, adjacent to Kittery (kit-tree), which is Maine's oldest. When a visitor to Maine comes over the interstate bridge from New Hampshire, on US Route 95, he will soon see ahead of him a conspicuous hill. This is Mount Agamenticus in the town of York. The hill is not over seven hundred feet high, but being surrounded by flat land, it looks taller. From the sea it looks still taller, and from earliest days has been used as a navigational aid. From the slope of Mount Agamenticus a small stream flows seaward and becomes tidal. The meadowland here is attractive, and in 1613 Captain John Smith saw the place and gave it a name on his map.

Captain Smith put a lot of places on his map that weren't there, but for a good reason. His map would be used back in England to entice settlers, and if he showed a few towns on his map, it would make people think somebody lived there. Captain Smith accordingly gave the coast of Maine several towns that didn't exist, and with whimsical touch he gave them good English names.

Where the Agamenticus River flows into the ocean he made a dot and called it Boston. Years would pass until in 1641 the Plymouth Company would cause a settlement there—the borough of Agamenticus.

The good English word "borough" was applied to several Maine communities which otherwise would pass as towns. Nobleborough, Waldoborough, Scarborough, Vassalborough, Jonesborough, Vanceborough, Waterborough, Pownalborough. Except for Scarborough, which still happily persists in full, the shorter "boro" came into custom with the establishment of the postal system, saving hundreds of barrels of ink each year. Thus, the post office of Waldoboro is in the town of Waldoborough, but who cares?

Earliest communities were chartered by England, but later the Massachusetts Bay Company assumed that authority. After 1680 the General Court of Massachusetts took over until 1820, and then Maine became its own state and the Maine legislature was in charge. All Maine minor civil divisions are "townships," signifying merely that the land has been surveyed and the area is designated on a map. The form of government bestowed when a township is organized and incorporated makes the differences as to "plantation," "town," and "city." Portland is a city; Freeport is a town; Monhegan Island is a plantation—all are townships. So Agamenticus was set up as a "borough" and remained so for some years.

Sir Ferdinando Gorges remains the patron saint of Maine, and at one time owned all of New England. His Plymouth Company enjoyed the favor of King Charles I, with whom Sir Ferdinando was chummy. The first effort of Gorges to settle "planters" in Maine was a failure, but in the next few decades he had more success. He never saw the lands given him by the Crown. He meant to come to Maine, but a vessel being readied for the voyage toppled on the stocks, and before repairs were finished Gorges died. His death came before his patron, Charles 1, was eliminated.

In 1641 Gorges established the borough of Agamenticus, and about that time he was beginning to have doubts about the continuation of his enterprises. It's a sad thing when a family "runs out," and Gorges seemed to feel that his son, his nephews, and his cousin were not tall timber. He thus thought to set himself up some sort of living monument, and he meditated on his borough of Agamenticus. So he issued a new charter, changing the status of Agamenticus to a "city" and changing the name to Gorgeana. Here his name would live on, and the situation (so his agents said) was propitious for future prosperity. The very first city in the New World thus came into being. Gorgeana was designated the capital of the Province of Maine. Gorges sent his cousin Thomas Gorges to be Mayor of Gorgeana and Deputy Governor of The Maine. Provision was made for a mansion, where Cousin Thomas lived in more than comfort.

The premonition of Sir Ferdinando that his heirs might be found wanting appears to have been justified. Shortly the citizens of Gorgeana shifted allegiance and elected one Edward Godfrey mayor. He would be Gorgeana's last mayor. By this time Massachusetts was on the rise, and there came the "oath of submission." Somewhat like the ancient governor of Capua who surrendered his city to the Romans, Mayor Godfrey of Gorgeana signed over to Massachusetts and put the skids under Sir Ferdinando. True, in later years the Crown ordered the Gorges lands to be returned to the Gorges heirs, but they immediately sold them to Massachusetts. The

Boston boys reduced the grandeur of Gorgeana City to a plain old "town," and in 1652 both Agamenticus and Gorgeana disappeared forever in favor of the name of York.

York was never derived from Quack, but came from Yorkshire in England, the home of white roses and the haggard ridings—north, east, and west. Yorkshire sent many settlers to Maine. Later, York, Maine, was to become shire town of York County in Maine, but in favor of a more central place York gave up this honor to nearby Alfred. In the archives of the York County Courthouse at Alfred are the oldest continuous judicial records in the country—among them the charter by which Sir Ferdinando Gorges created America's first "city," Gorgeana. It is at least amusing to conjecture if Gorgeana would have done better as Quack.

Having taken care of America's first city, in the same historical breath we might as well give heed to America's biggest "town." As we've seen, the size and population of a Maine township has nothing to do with its kind of government. Accordingly, it is not at all odd (in Maine) that Madawaska as a town was three and a half times the size of Rhode Island and nine and a half times the size of Los Angeles. The history of Madawaska began before anybody in Maine knew it was there. It was a fief granted in 1683 by the French governor of Canada to Sieur Charles-Aubert de Chenaye, who sold it in 1763 to General James Murray, governor of Quebec. The original boundaries of this fief were in keeping with the township size of the times, a little more than thirty-six square miles. But the whole thing was speculative because nobody lived there, and since the area was remote it would be a long time until somebody did. The first settlers were Acadians from Nova Scotia who were exiled

by the English in 1755. They came up the St. John
River to a closer haven, rather than endure the long
Evangeline route through the Great Lakes and down
the Mississippi River to Louisiana. Daigles, Fourniers,
Cyrs, Thibodeaux, Duperres, they cut out farms and
settled in to become a completely French community
on the tip-top hump of Maine, lost in the woods. French
is still a handy thing to have in Madawaska.

But the size of the "town" of Madawaska was a consequence of the approach of the Aroostook War. Maine,
newly become a state, was feeling friction along the
northern boundary. Timber, rather than farmland, was
the thrust. Maine lumbermen were howling at the statehouse to gain protection from the dirty English and their
knavish tricks. Timber thieves, they shouted, were the
ruination of prosperity. Canadians were poaching the
pine and spruce. The downstate legislature thereupon
incorporated (1831) the town of Madawaska and included
in the territory anything and everything that anybody
could think of, just to be on the safe side. This was,
admittedly, "a continued assertion of the right of the
state to jurisdiction over the territory known to be within
the limits of Maine." The good people of Madawaska
hadn't petitioned for anything so assertive or so thorough and didn't know they were so prosperous, but the
lumber barons who fomented the big claim saw to it
that the incorporation was consummated. Shortly a town
meeting was held and officers elected and the biggest
town in the New World was in business. A month later
a second meeting elected a representative to the Maine
legislature.

This election gummed things up, and revealed the
incorporation of the town of Madawaska as the flimflam
it was. Peter Lizotte was the winner in the election, and

immediately he wrote a letter to Governor Samuel Smith down at the statehouse to say he would not qualify and would not serve. He said he was a British subject and hoped to live the rest of his days and die as such. Under no circumstances would he swear allegiance to the United States or to the State of Maine. So *that* Madawaska never did send a representative down to legislature at Augusta, and Governor Smith was obliged to admit that the whole Madawaska caper had an ulterior purpose and he questioned the ethics. But that incorporation of Madawaska was never repealed and remained a lawful subterfuge for thirty-eight years.

In 1869, after the boundary disputes had been settled and the Aroostook War was well over, the incorporation of Madawaska had a rerun, and this time its size was whittled down to a mere 38,000 acres—quite a comedown from the 4,272 square miles that made Madawaska the largest community in North America. And some of those 38,000 acres are bog and swamp. All of today's Madawaska lies in Maine, but from most doorsteps there may be seen the long miles of that first Madawaska that lie over in Canada. The St. John River is beautiful and here is some of Maine's most salubrious scenery. In Micmac Indian, Madawaska means "place of the ducks in the reeds of the island in the river."

32

Something of how things went in the early days of Maine towns, with an amusing recitation frequently heard as to why the village blacksmith often did his work, as in Longfellow's poem, under the spreading chestnut tree.

It was reasonable for Europeans to come and settle along the Maine coast—the ocean gave them jobs and there was beauty in their surroundings. But what folly prompted folks to move up into the Maine forests to starve on rocky acres where—as was said of the Town of Bowdoin—the soil was so poor that a load of manure had to be put in a man's grave so his soul could rise? Some few, we know, went into the woods to get away from the ocean. Such as the seven families from Martha's Vineyard who wanted a haven from the perils and hardships of life by the sea. They could have picked the lush valleys of the Sandy and Carrabasset Rivers, the best farmland in Maine, but they didn't want even that much water in their new careers, so they went up on New Vineyard Mountain to pick rocks and grind sheep. Grind sheep—that's a Maine saying. Farmers had to hold their sheep's noses to a grindstone to sharpen them off so the poor things could pick grass between rocks.

Timber did attract, but the downright harvest of logs that was "to let daylight into the swamps" was some time ahead of the first settlers. One early reason for upland settlers was the grant of farmland to revolutionary veterans—Massachusetts gave of her public lands in the District of Maine to men who had fought the British. The manner of granting these bonus lands was casual enough so some nonveterans became Mainers, and there was at least one "veteran" who neglected to explain to the authorities that he had fought on the other side.

This is true; in a small country cemetery in Androscoggin County is the grave of a "first settler," a man who came to take up a farm as his right after service. His descendants are numerous enough in the area so it would be indiscreet to set his name down here. As a soldier of the revolution he was respected and honored into his late years, and his grave was suitably marked. It was after the American Legion had taken over the Grand Army's annual decoration of soldiers' graves that a great-great-great-granddaughter of this pioneer got curious and looked up his military record. He did not appear in the Massachusetts Militia, and he was not on the roll of the Continental army. A tedious search found that he had been a Redcoat, and at Bunker Hill had sustained a broken leg when the patriots rolled down a barrel of rocks. But be not dismayed—his grave is still marked and gets Memorial Day attention every year.

As to enticing innocent victims otherwise, an answer is in the way townships were made available with the condition of settlement. The present town of Garland, for instance, was in 1796 designated by the surveyors as Township Number Three in the Fifth Range north of the Waldo Patent. As such, it was given by the General Court of Massachusetts to the trustees of the newly founded Williams College. The college had full power to convey and dispose of the land, proceeds to be used for its educational purposes. Bowdoin College in Maine was at the same time established and received a similar grant of land. These grants carried the requirement that a certain number of families should be settled in the township designated within so many years, and also stipulated that three lots be reserved—one lot for the first settled minister, one to support his church, and the third for a school. In Township 3–5 these lots had 350 acres each.

The quickest way for Williams College to get any money out of this was to turn the land over to a promoter, and by the merest coincidence one happened to be ready and willing with the money in hand. He was one Levi Lincoln. Mr. Lincoln was well-to-do and looking for an investment, and afterwards became governor of Massachusetts and more well-to-do. He handed $2,500 to the trustees of Williams College, agreed to develop the township, and thus came to own 23,040 acres of good farmland and valuable timber. As "proprietor," he began at once to turn a profit, and his first step was to induce six families to move up to 3–5 and clear land. To tempt them, he kept his prices down, so for maybe five dollars a man could own a couple of hundred acres. But Mr. Lincoln shrewdly sent on ahead an "agent" who sewed up the best water-power site. Mr. Lincoln never stepped on 3–5, but for some years the place was known as Lincolntown. In a few years 3–5 had the required clearings, and while Mr. Lincoln was happy, Williams College soon spent its $2,500 and started an alumni fund.

The nucleus of original settlers, having opened the wilderness and built trails and roads under something of a subsidy, was soon joined by others who paid longer prices for their land. For many years to come there would be an annual roundup of animals and a shipment of grains and shingles and whatever else would help pay Mr. Lincoln the interest on his notes.

The "reserved lots" continue in fact to the present. Edward Everett Hale wrote a short story called "My Double and How He Undid Me," which is worth reading for itself, but it also tells how one of these "ministerial lots" was taken up. A Massachusetts minister, victim of his own conniving, is unable to face the consequences, and retreats to a wilderness township in Maine to claim his free lot. As the "first settled minister" he was entitled to it, although there was no church. The income from "church lots" caused some confusion in townships where several creeds claimed it, but so far the United States Supreme Court wouldn't touch this church-and-state situation with a ten-foot pole.

As soon as the "proprietor" got enough people settled into his grant, there was need of services, and every town dutifully welcomed its first minister, its first cobbler, its first blacksmith, its first miller, its first doctor, its first schoolmaster. Those settlers on New Vineyard Mountain made a deal with one Chesley Pinkham, miller, and agreed to support him if he would bring his wheel to grind their grain and saw their boards. A dam was built on a small stream tributary to the Carrabasset River, and Chesley was soon in business. He got all the trade from the New Vineyard settlers, and folks at a distance were bringing him work.

Chesley became the most prosperous man in the settlement, as he got his miller's share of every bag of meal and every bolt of shingles. But in those times money was seldom seen, and Chesley had to take his goods down-country to sell for cash. At first, although United States dollars were now coin of the realm, these upland Maine people still talked in shillings, and Chesley came to have quite a few. When he was older, and after gold coinage was established, Chesley Pinkham put all his fortune into double eagles—an eagle was the ten-dollar gold coin, and the double eagle was worth twenty. Lacking a bank, Chesley went down under the timbers of his mill when he was alone and bored auger holes into the joists. He'd poke his double eagles into a hole until the hole was full, and then he'd pound in a wooden plug. Nobody knew about this except Chesley, so nobody now knows how many holes he had. One spring a flash flood ripped down off the mountain, taking out Chesley's dam and distributing his mill timber by timber for miles down the valley.

For the remainder of his life Chesley wandered up and down the banks of that stream hoping to find some timbers with plugs in auger holes. Since he didn't tell why, he was considered crazy in the head and became a legend. But not long before he died he explained his search, and after that a good many people also became "crazy in the head" and wandered up and down the stream. The right timbers from Chesley's mill have not been found. Yet.

Several Maine towns share a common story about the arrival of a first blacksmith. No doubt some one town owns the story, but which? The trade of ironworker was by no means something to take lightly. An anvil isn't something a man picks up and carries into the wilderness just like that. The raw materials are heavy, and the nailrods needed could crack a wagon axle. A bag of Tynecoal would tire any horse on a woods trail. Meantime, every settlement needed shoes for horses and oxen, and nails and sled runners, and varmint traps and axes. Which means that when a blacksmith did arrive, he had a summer's work ahead of him before he got a roof up. Almost every "first" blacksmith seems to have set up his business under a spreading chestnut tree, and left the building of a shop until the rush slackened. The first blacksmiths worked outdoors.

So a stranger was riding along one time and his horse threw a shoe and went lame. There the stranger was, knowing only that some trees had spots on them, and in his perplexity he was right happy to look up and see a man walking towards him. After the amenities, the stranger said, "I don't suppose they's any such thing in this country as a blacksmith shop?"

"Yes, they is," said the man. "You're standing in it this minute—but the forge is four miles up the trail."

33

Making a memorial rather to
Game Warden Stephen Powell
than to Colonel Benedict Arnold,
but mentioning both, and
dwelling on Canabais Princess
Jacataqua, very pretty, who shot a
bear.

Statistically, the people of the United States have always been thoughtlessly harsh on Benedict Arnold.
Thoughtlessly, because we've never meditated fairly on
the circumstances and conditions that prevailed in his
time, the frustrations he experienced, and particularly
the military politics that prevailed in the army of Good
General Washington. Benedict Arnold was a captain of
militia in his home colony of Connecticut when he heard
about the doings at Concord and Lexington, and he
immediately brought his company to Cambridge. He
advanced to major general, and was an astute and able

officer, possibly as keen as anybody on Washington's staff. He was a colonel, and in excellent repute, when he arrived in Maine in the fall of 1775 to lead an expedition against British-held Quebec City.

Arnold had proposed early on that the Revolutionary War might be sooner ended if the British supply line up the St. Lawrence River and into New York could be cut off. Ethan Allen and his Green Mountain Boys had made a start. Now, an army would follow the ancient Indian trail up Maine's Kennebec River, over the Height of Land, and down to the St. Lawrence to take Quebec. It was a reasonable proposition, by no means an impossible mission, and Colonel Benedict Arnold was considered the right man for the job. Much that turned this effort into a disaster deserves the meditation suggested above, and in one of the Bigger IF's of History, we may well wonder about Benedict Arnold had he succeeded at Quebec.

Be that as it may, Colonel Arnold was in no disrepute whatever when his ten transports came down from Newburyport and sailed up the Kennebec River on the first leg of his long march through Maine and into Canada. He came to Merrymeeting Bay, where five rivers come together—the Kennebec, the Androscoggin, the Cathance, the Abbagadusset, and the Muddy. And he came to Swan Island, just above Merrymeeting Bay, which divides the Kennebec into two channels and had for some five thousand years been a winter community for the Kennebec, or Canabais, Indians. Swan Island has some two and a half square miles, and today is a game management preserve of the Maine Department of Inland Fisheries and Wildlife. The preserve is named to honor Stephen Powell, a Maine game warden and wildlife biologist who retired after long and dedicated service, only to die much too soon.

When Benedict Arnold and his men touched at Swan Island in October of 1775, the Kennebec Indians had pretty much come downstream from their summer hunting grounds, and at the time their chief was their Princess Jacataqua, who lingers in Maine lore as a beautiful, intelligent, friendly female such as hadn't graced high position since Cleopatra. She welcomed Colonel Benedict Arnold, and went so far as to offer her services as guide for the rest of the trip—an offer that was not accepted, although several Kennebecs did guide the expedition.

It chanced that one of the younger officers on Arnold's staff was a good-looking fellow named Aaron Burr. The same. He would one day become vice president of the United States, and it was he who had the duel with Alexander Hamilton. At Swan Island Aaron Burr was not yet encumbered with too many military duties, and Arnold's men were in good spirits and not yet burdened by the hard journey ahead. There was time for dalliance. Aaron Burr took one look at Princess Jacataqua and she took one look at Aaron Burr, and a romance ensued. And one afternoon when the two were alone with their thoughts, an opportunity offered and Princess Jacataqua shot a black bear. The princess then performed her squaw work of skinning the beast, dressing it out, and cutting the meat, after which they returned to the Indian village. This led to a great feast. The princess had the bear roasted, and all of Colonel Benedict Arnold's men and all the Kennebec Indians joined in a banquet to celebrate the departure to Quebec, and to promote joviality and common disport.

Swan Island became a game management preserve because people insist on picking up fawns along in June and July when they are newly born. The mother doe will trot away a short distance if she hears something she doesn't like, but will return when all is well. People who find a fawn foolishly assume it has been abandoned, and in spite of repeated warnings by game wardens to let "abandoned" fawns alone, every summer such fawns are brought to game wardens with many a "poor-itty-bitty-thing!" and the game wardens all over Maine were spending a lot of time with nursing bottles. Warden Steve Powell suggested these fawns be brought to him at Swan Island, where he could fetch them up on a wholesale basis.

Swan Island also became a recovery place for all kinds of game that got injured, but not enough to be destroyed. A deer hit by an automobile would be taken to Swan Island to have a broken leg fixed. Later, deer duly tagged in one ear as a Swan Island graduate would be trucked deep into the wilderness and released. Swan Island came to have so many deer Warden Powell had to cut and store hay to feed them. By arrangement, visitors were ferried across the narrow channel from Richmond Village, and Steve Powell put on a great show as he entertained them.

Steve was a huge man, and would hang out over the gunwales of a canoe. But he was agile and light on his feet, and one of his tricks was to dash into the woods of Swan Island and come out carrying a fawn to show the visitors close up. In addition to the wildlife, Steve's entertainment included all the lore and legends of the Indian days. He had many stone weapons and some pieces of pottery he had found on Swan Island, and one of his better monologues had to do with Aaron Burr, Princess Jacataqua, and how they killed a bear and put on a banquet.

Warden Stephen Powell's long career as manager of the Swan Island Game management program was interrupted once when he went back to school. Every summer the fish and game commissioner would arrange seminars, or a refresher course, and assign fifteen game wardens to attend and improve themselves. Accordingly, it became Steve's turn, and he was told to go to the University of Maine at Orono and attend a two-week session devoted to the study of statistics and how they may be applied to game management matters. It had been many years since Steve had earned his B.S. from the university, and he had misgivings about going back to school—for one thing, he wondered if he could get his great bulk into a lecture hall seat-desk. After Steve got back from that session, he incorporated his experiences into his talks to Swan Island visitors. His recitations had to do with basic, down-to-earth, realistic facts coming up head-on against the ephemeral, whimsical, theoretical, and quaint notions of the professional professor.

For a starter, Steve would explain how the professor introduced his subject by asking each man to make a list of one thousand selected random numbers. At this, Steve raised his hand and asked what would be random about selected numbers. He said the professor gave him a double-talk answer that nobody understood, and after that the professor would give a little start every so often, shudder, and look up at Steve and wag his head. For the next class, the professor had everybody flip a coin a thousand times and jot down the heads and tails. Steve said the funniest thing he ever saw in his life was a roomful of uniformed game wardens flipping coins— utterly absorbed in the magic of statistics.

Then the class began to take samples and project them into statistical conclusions. Steve used to say he counted 5,299 deer legs and proved there was a three-legged deer in Allagash Plantation. Things like that. He sampled 300,000 Canada Geese at Merrymeeting Bay, interpolated the wetlands factor, corrected for forage deficiencies, and projected by statistics that every playground in the City of Portland had twelve geese.

It was Princess Jacataqua who gave Warden Stephen Powell his best monologue. He would relate how Benedict Arnold came with his men, comment that the man got the dirty end of a stick and describe Jacataqua in every detail of her beauty, charm, and friendly nature. He dwelt on Aaron Burr, and he told about the bear. He led his visitors to the very place where the Indian village had a stone fireplace; the very spot where this black bear had been roasted to regale the army of Arnold and the Kennebecs. Steve would say, "And by simple statistics I can prove that a black bear that will feed eleven hundred hungry soldiers and three hundred eager Indians will stand eighty-five feet tall."

34

The story of Father Rasle is included, but it is not a pretty tale, and any good history of Maine would be better still without it, but in those days nobody was above reproach, and let the chips fall.

There's nothing comical in the career of the late Father Sebastian Rasle of Norridgewock, unless perhaps there's a smile about his name. Of the two and twenty ways to spell it—Rale, Rassle, Ralleais, Rallé, and so on—the monument to his memory at Indian Old Point uses Rasle. That was the preference of no less an authority than Bishop Benedict Fenwick of Boston, who had the monument erected in 1833, one hundred and nine years after Rasle had been methodically done in by the English colonists who thought they'd put up with quite enough of his kind of "religion."

Sebastian Rasle was born a French gentleman, and as a Jesuit priest came to Canada to make converts of the savage Indians. He was one of a succession of such priests who authored the *Jesuit Relations*, which historians love to quote, and which tell us so much about our Red Men. Maine had reasonably gentle experiences with Fathers Biard, Massé, and Thury, who had labored amongst the Micmacs and Penobscots, but when Father Rasle was sent to bring Christian light to the Kennebecs he introduced some new techniques that hardly endeared him to the English folks who were trying to make a living along The Maine. The others led lives of quiet inspiration, but Rasle came later and was here in the hectic years of the early eighteenth century. Father Rasle used his priesthood, the Christian religion, and the Roman Catholic Church to keep his "converts" on the warpath against the English—something not histori- cally dissociated from the Jesuit custom. He told his Indians, after he had them sufficiently converted, that Mary, Mother of Jesus, was a French lady, and that the English had murdered her baby.

Sebastian Rasle has persisted as a righteous, selfless, dedicated, pious missionary devoted to good deeds, exuding the divinity that doth hedge a priest. He per- sisted as such even after some of his letters to a nephew in France were found—letters that revealed him other- wise. But to the English in Maine during the early 1700s, Father Rasle was a scheming rascal, even though they knew nothing about those letters. They weren't about to agree that a fine gentleman of the cloth was above reproach.

True, those early English settlers weren't above reproach themselves, and they couldn't blame all the Indian troubles on Father Rasle. Our ancestors hadn't

been all that righteous and diplomatic in dealing with
the natives, and just deserts are still just deserts. But
there had been a lull, and when the Indians began to
ravage the settlements again, with a new kind of inten-
sity, the influence of Father Rasle wasn't hard to recognize.

The Indians who lived along the Kennebec River were
a family of the Etchimins known as the Canabais. They
were somewhat advanced of other northeastern tribes,
more like the Tarratines of the Penobscot, with whom
they associated. They lived in substantial houses and
could send messages by pictures, and they were not so
warlike as tribes to the westward. By the time Father
Rasle came to convert them, the Canabais had dwindled
considerably, partly because many had migrated north-
ward to join the refugee "St. Francis" tribe. Some, too,
had moved over to be with the Penobscots. The village
of the Canabais at Indian Old Point, now part of the
Town of Madison, was their upstream home, at the
junction of the Kennebec River and Sandy Stream—a
spot idyllic, Downstream, the Canabais would winter
at Swan Island.

It was to Indian Old Point that Father Rasle came to
redeem the heathen and endear them to him. He was
already conversant in other Indian tongues, and soon
was fluent in Canabais—he produced a dictionary that
Harvard now treasures, and for his church services
translated hymns into Canabais. He preached in that
tongue. His chapel was a timbered structure, with a
steeple able to stand the rocking of a sixty-pound bell
brought from France. The bell is now with the Maine
Historical Society at Portland, and possibly an occasional visitor will wonder how it came from France, and
how it was brought down from Quebec. Who toted it

over the Height of Land? Did it come down Dead River, or was it taken to the Rangeleys and then down Sandy Stream? What did the Canabais Indians think of it? The church had paintings of the Crucifixion and other biblical scenes, and Father Rasle had a silver service for his alter. All was pleasing to the Indians, and they rallied with enthusiasm to the Gospel according to Rasle.

Father Rasle wrote to his nephew that he found it necessary to "fix the imagination of these savages," and he told how he used the pageantry of the mass to gain and hold their attention. He made a morning mass and then had vespers, and everybody came. The children said their catechism. Forty men, he wrote, formed a choir, and sang with good voice. Each proudly wore a surplice. His acolytes assisted, even to ringing the bell. So it would be hard to believe that this holy man had other than holy thoughts and holy purposes.

As things worsened and Father Rasle's Indians were making forays against the English settlements on the coast, there was an attempt to reason with him. The Governor of Massachusetts sent a letter, but when Father Rasle answered it he overlooked the purpose of the message and found fault with the governor's Latin. Somewhat haughtily, in fact, and not as befits a French gentleman of culture. Harvard used better Latin then than did the Vatican. The governor was not amused. And Father Rasle continued to encourage his doting Indians from his pleasant pulpit at Old Point.

Fort George at Thomaston was attacked; several English were killed. At Casco a lone English settler was dropped in his tracks by a musket ball from the woods. Three Englishmen coming ashore in a boat never knew what hit them. Father Rasle well knew the situation in Europe with England and France, and he knew the importance of land in America, but he didn't have to explain all that to his choirboys. They'd come out of the woods, raise havoc, and be gone back to Indian Old Point to sing in church.

In July of 1722 the legislature of Massachusetts, having had no serious reply to overtures for peace, declared war on the Indians as enemies of the king. But the Indians didn't present anything much to make war against. They'd appear at odd places at odd times, and British definitions of declared war hardly helped. But Father Rasle was recognized for what he was, and an expedition to exterminate him and his choirboys was favored. A bounty of one thousand livres was offered for his scalp, and when a squad of Englishmen arrived at Old Point the place was deserted—the Indians and Father Rasle had skedaddled. With good British gallantry the village was spared and the soldiers went home, so shortly Father Rasle was back in business.

In 1724 the Indians came on again. They killed more than thirty people in a few weeks; a good many of the victims were sitting ducks. One man was just enjoying the sun on his doorstep when he got a ball in the head. At Kennebunk three men were surprised while working a sawmill, and their scalps went to Old Point. At Berwick two small boys were devoutly dispatched: one had his skull knocked in and the other was left to die— bleeding, gasping, and scalped. Two fishing boats in the St. George River were ambushed and sixteen men perished miserably as they stepped ashore.

So things were going all along The Maine and like Carthage, Father Rasle had to be destroyed. Two hundred and eight men, guided by Mohawks, left Swan Island and started up the Kennebec towards Indian Old Point. They had careful instructions, incapable of being

misunderstood, that Father Rasle was not to be harmed.
The expedition succeeded. This time the Canabais had
no warning, and the initial English attack took care of
things nicely. Not an Englishman was hurt. When Father
Rasle came from his chapel, carrying a cross and surrounded protectively by his acolytes, he was mowed
down, and so were the acolytes. The village was burned.
Years later the chapel bell was found under ashes.

Immediately, of course, good Father Rasle became an
abused saint, a righteous Catholic priest done in by the
black Protestants of Boston. This estimation of the man
persisted, and strengthened, even after his revealing letters to his nephew were found in France. It persists even
now. It is supported considerably by the monument
Bishop Fenwick erected to Rasle's memory in 1883. The
inscription is ironically in Boston Latin, but it calls Rasle
"this best of pastors," and his converts "his deceased
Children in Christ." The attack not only took care of
Father Rasle, but rather much brought an end to the
Canabais Indians. A few joined the Penobscots, and
others went up to St. Francis preserves. Most died at
Indian Old Point.

And Bishop Fenwick, memorializing Father Rasle,
gave no thought whatever to erecting any monuments
along the coast of Maine to the memory of hundreds of
State-o'-Mainers who had been massacred by these
innocent Children of Christ—until their best of pastors
was liquidated.

35

A short study of the difference between the local parish and the church it supported, explaining why the good reverend, pastor of the church, was not always privileged to arise and speak.

Now and then curious tourists will ask about Maine's "parish" churches. The sign will say:

First Parish Church
Congregational

So, why not the First Congregational Church? The town of Freeport is a good place to examine this question, where the First Parish Church stands in the bustle and clutter of Freeport's modern business, an attractive edifice retaining some of the town's earlier charm. The church, by the way, still uses a true pipe organ, having resisted the general impulse to go electronic, albeit an electrically powered blower was installed some years back to replace what the ancient parish records called "boy to pump." Said boy provided the wind for the pipes by working a lever up and down and was paid, according to those records, twenty-five cents a Sunday. Practice sessions on "choir night" (Thursdays), when the organist and choir got ready for Sundays, earned him nothing extra.

As a part of very old North Yarmouth, Freeport's earliest activities belong in the North Yarmouth history, but by 1789 the community had enough people to go it alone, and was set off as Maine's sixty-fourth town. There had been harbor activity for years, and in the area there had been a church for some time—the typical meeting house handling both civic and spiritual gatherings as a consequence of the Boston influence. Boston recognized only church members as citizens.

But by this time certain "odd ones" were being recognized, and Maine tended to be more liberal than Massachusetts, so as the Freeport charter was arranged, thought was given to Baptists and Universalists—and even Methodists. Freeport was thus set up as a town, first, and then a parish for church purposes. Citizenship in the town was willy-nilly, but membership in the parish was elective. Baptists, rightfully, should not be expected to support the Congregational church. Under this dual arrangement Freeport did business for many years in sweet serenity and had no problems. Every March there would be a town meeting when citizens gathered to elect officers, appropriate money, and decide on policy. Then, a week or so later, the members of the parish (and for the most part the same people) would assemble to take care of the church business.

The first church had been down on the road to Porter's Landing, and by 1818 was too small. It was torn down and a second church started up in the village. This one caught fire before it was finished, and a third effort was made on the same foundation. And, later, the present little church on lower Main Street was built. So the present Congregational Church with its pipe organ is the fourth that the "first parish" has had. It survives in that context in pleasant contrast to the "other" churches in town—the First Baptist, the now-vacant Universalist, and the latter-day Roman Catholic. But, true enough, almost all of this is misted in memory, seldom brought to mind, and the Congregationalists have even yielded their prestigious preference to something called the Church of Christ—fairly far from any parochial context. Doubtless most faithful Freeporters haven't the foggiest suspicion that they ever belonged to a parish.

But there was one high moment in the history of Freeport's first parish that should be forever remembered.

It was in the 1920s. Freeport was Freeport then, and not open twenty-four hours a day. There were still people in town who knew about the separation of church and state; who knew the difference between a town and a parish—and more than that, people who knew the difference between the church and the parish. There were Freeporters who didn't belong to the parish, and there were those who belonged to the parish but didn't belong to the church. So it happened quite naturally that a faithful attendant at the church, who was not a member of the church, nonetheless was elected treasurer of the parish. All proper and lawful. He entered upon his duties with purpose, determined to do a good job, because at the moment the church was in need of support. Many who had pledged were delinquent in dropping their envelopes into the basket, and the treasurer was having a difficult time paying the bills. The pastor hadn't been paid, for instance. So this new non-church-member did his best as treasurer of the parish to drum up enough dollars to put the house in order. He dunned the back-sliders, but this didn't suffice, so he took his parish books and climbed the stairs to call on Mr. L.L. Bean.

In the 1920s Mr. Bean was not yet the internationally famous mail-order tycoon, but he was on his way, and he was all the same a successful local businessman. The parish treasurer showed him the books with a bank balance of $9.35 and said, "So dammit, L.L., we got to bail the old church out!"

It was a fact, and on record, that Mrs. Bean was indeed a member of that church, and had been faithful with her pledge envelopes, but now her husband said, "But why *me*, Frank? Don't tell me your grief—I don't belong to the goddam church."

To which, because of the dual situation that prevailed, the treasurer of the parish answered, "I know that—neither do I." This logic prevailed, and Mr. L. L. Bean made a substantial contribution which, incidentally, he matched every year after that. The treasurer of the parish then made out a check for the minister's back pay, and went across the street to pay the church's coal bill. This shows us how the parish served the purpose of keeping the church in good shape.

And it so happened a few years later that the time came for the annual parish meeting, and the warrant notifying members was posted, like Luther's theses, on the door of the church. At the stated time the members of the parish arrived, elected a moderator, and business began. Things went smoothly for a time, and then the minister of the church arose and said, "Mr. Moderator!"

The moderator naturally responded, "The chair recognizes our pastor!" But before the minister got three words out, the aforementioned treasurer of the parish stood up and said, "I rise to a point of order!"

The moderator properly said, "Please state your point of order!"

The treasurer of the parish said, "You've recognized the gentleman and given him the floor—but he's not a member of this parish."

The moderator did his best. He said, "But—he's our pastor!" A remark which gratuitously extended courtesy to the cloth.

"I know that," said the treasurer. "But it don't make no damn's odds who he is if he don't belong. Look at the bylaws. The gentleman is a resident of New Hampshire, and won't qualify in this parish for four more months. No way he can speak in this meeting except by unanimous consent."

The moderator tried again. "But surely—you don't mean to silence our own minister, do you?"

"I just want to make the point that he isn't a member of our parish."

"But he's the minister of our church!"

"True, and that makes him a hired man, and it's the parish that hires him. The minute the church begins running the parish, we're in trouble."

"But I think we should hear his remarks."

"Maybe we should—so I ask for unanimous consent to hear the gentleman's remarks."

The moderator sighed dramatically—big fuss over nothing—and intoned, "Unanimous consent is asked to hear the gentleman."

The correct parliamentary manner with a motion for unanimous consent is to call for the negatives. It takes only one to defeat the motion, so there is no point in ascertaining the number in favor. The moderator said, "Do I hear a no?"

The treasurer of the parish said, "No!"

Then, having made his point, he rose once again to offer his resignation as treasurer of the parish. "I never belonged to this church," he said, "but I've sure as hell carried my weight as a member of the parish. I can see the time has come when all of us need to take notice of just what that means. This parish can sell the damn church if it wants to—we might even decide to turn it into a hotel. Not that we will. But the way things are going, we might bear that in mind—we still owe our minister three weeks' pay."

But the treasurer (retired) lost the battle. People who had forgotten about the ancient distinction of church and parish found the incident regrettable and an affront to a good man of the faith. Plans were soon afoot to eliminate the parish, and as more and more folks forgot the town's deep roots in a congregational past, it was soon accomplished. Then the Congregational persuasion embraced the Church of Christ, and an era ended. So far, the lovely little church in Freeport has not been turned into a hotel.

36

Captain Lovewell (pronounced lovell) has his story told once more, this time without the glitter and glamour lavished on it previously by imaginative narrators who abused the rigid rules of truth outrageously.

"History," said General Burgoyne (in *The Devil's Disciple* of George Bernard Shaw) "will tell lies." A dandy sample of historical prevarication is found in the accounts of Lovewell's War, to which Maine schoolchildren have been subjected over the years on the grounds that Captain John Lovewell was a brave soldier, a distinguished gentleman, a devout Christian, an able commander, and a man of upright character. When veracity is encouraged, things look otherwise. When the balderdash is seasoned with facts, things run this way:

King Philip had been decorously done away with,

along with most of his people, and the expedition to
Norridgewock had ruined the Kennebec Indians and
neatly eliminated the troublesome Father Rasle. The so-
called French and Indian Wars were tapering off. But
when the men returned from teaching Father Rasle a
good lesson, they had eighty scalps they had lifted in
the manly encounter, and would any good little boy or
girl care to raise a hand and tell us what a scalp was
worth? Captain Harmon set his men at ease at Richmond, after coming back from Norridgewock, and took
those scalps to Boston. The good and godly people of
Boston greeted him as a conquering hero, paid him the
bounty, promoted him to lieutenant colonel, and lent
him two horses so he could return to Maine with the
money.

Thus prosperity accrued, and there followed what is
sometimes called the Fourth Indian War in 1722. It is
also called, at other times, Three Years of Lovewell's
War—an exercise that made good use of the scalp bounty
in Boston. In the beginning the native eastern Indians,
being hunters, fishers, and tillers, weren't much given
to lifting scalps, and at times they deplored the custom
as encouraged by the settlers. This Captain John Lovewell was from Dunstable, down in Christian Massachusetts, and he liked scalping. In December of 1722 he
signed up thirty men as a company of militia and led
them on an Indian hunt in the Lake Winnipesaukee
region. The Sokokis Indians had used that area as
camping and hunting grounds for generations, and it
happened at the time they were not unduly mad at any
settlers. Indeed, they were disposed to trade and were
personally acquainted with many Englishmen. At least
the Sokokis were not expecting to be abused. But they
all had scalps.

Now along comes Captain Lovewell, full of patriotism and military ardor, with his thirty men, and the
party comes upon an Indian. With this Indian is a small
boy, also an Indian. By combining their patriotic ardor
and their military skills, the thirty men succeeded in
killing the Indian and the little boy, and the two scalps
were worth two hundred pounds in Boston—not a bad
day's work for a bunch of Christians otherwise unemployed.

The next year, having learned a good deal about Indian
warfare by this experience, Captain Lovewell did much
better. This time he took forty men and off they went
in the same general direction, coming at last to a small
pond of the Salmon Falls River headwaters, and there
by the greatest good chance they came upon an Indian
camp. Ten braves had seemingly enjoyed a feast, and
now were sound asleep by their campfires in a surfeit
of good food. We now learn something about the
marksmanship of Captain Lovewell's men. The forty of
them drew deliberate aim, and as Captain Lovewell
lowered his arm they let go a simultaneous blast. In this
manner they killed nine of the ten Indians, which for
dead aim at ten paces is not championship scoring. The
tenth Indian, being awakened by the gunfire, jumped
up with the notion that he was being used in a rude and
uncouth manner, and he ran away.

Since Captain Lovewell had stupidly allowed all his
men to fire their guns at once, and since it took some
time to recharge the muskets of those days, all the forty
men could do was watch the Indian go, and the more
they watched the more he went. However, a dog attached
to the brave company took after the heathen savage and
sank his teeth in such a manner that the Indian was
restrained until the men could reach him and kill him

with their hatchets. The ten scalps were forwarded to Boston, to be redeemed for one thousand pounds, sterling. One historian says Captain Lovewell was given "universal applause" for his courageous action, but this other historian, here, says, "Quid non mortalia pectora cogis auri sacra fames!"

It's true that some Indians did keep pestering the settlers, often being needlessly abrupt and cruel, but it is also true that during Lovewell's little war no great distinction was made between good Indians and bad Indians. The next sortie of the gallant and fun-loving Lovewell points this up. This is the Pegwacket Ploy, to coin a term. Pegwacket was an Indian village in the Ossipee Lakes country, spelled some sixteen ways in older records but all pronounced pee-kwocket. It stood in a delightful intervale with fertile soil, romantic surroundings, and a sweetheart of a view. The Indians there, at the moment, were not mad at the English, and a good many of the menfolks were well acquainted with settlers along the Saco River. But friend or foe, Indians have scalps.

Captain Lovewell now organized another company— forty-six men tried and true and fully equipped. Moving up the Saco, he came to Great Ossipee Pond and built a stockade—a place of retreat if he met reverses, and also a field hospital for eight of his men, who had come down with the gollywobbles on the way up the river. Leaving the sick men, a surgeon, and a guard, Captain Lovewell now pushed forward with thirty-two men in hot pursuit of scalps. When approaching the village of Pegwacket he made camp for the night—just beyond a small lake that lies now in the town of Fryeburg and is called Lovewell's Pond. Here is the stone monument to his memory. The men now worked in complete silence, so near they were to the savage enemy, and Chaplain Jonathan Frye barely whispered when he conducted evening prayers. Captain Lovewell was pious, and always insisted on devotions and the Christian niceties.

In the morning, Chaplain Frye again led the prayers, and he was interrupted by a gunshot in the distance. Since Chaplain Frye was a graduate of Harvard College, this was an affront, and Captain Lovewell clenched his teeth and vowed vengeance. From the campsite an Indian could be seen along the shore on the other side of the pond—he was out looking for a bird and had just shot one. Since this Indian's scalp was worth five hundred dollars, Captain Lovewell immediately formed ranks and charged. As the men moved along they came upon an open space in the woods—a bosky dell green of grass and without underbrush, a happenstance in the otherwise dense forest. Captain Lovewell now demonstrated his high grade of military intelligence all over the place. He let the men discard their knapsacks, piling them in this delightful nook so they might move with ease through the forest. The packs would be retrieved on the return, and the bosky dell would be easy to find. Pay attention, one and all, for the best part comes next.

In a mile or so the soldiers came upon the Indian, who had a gun in one hand and a bird in the other. He was completely unaware of Captain Lovewell and his bold militiamen. He wasn't mad at anybody and was sauntering pleasantly in good spirit and with amiable disposition. His thoughts were, perhaps, on the joy his squaw would display as she made his bird ready for the pot. What was his surprise when thirty-two guns banged at him! Deeming this an unfriendly act, the Indian jumped behind a tree to look out at the thirty-two militiamen. Not one of them had hit his mark. Score: zero. Captain Lovewell clearly needed a firearms instructor. Now the Indian brought his own gun up and took a shot at Captain Lovewell. In that way Captain Lovewell was wounded—not seriously. By now the soldiers had their guns recharged, and one of them shot the Indian. They took his scalp, and with Captain Lovewell's wound dressed, the party retraced. They would pick up their knapsacks at the sylvan glen.

But alas and gadzooks! A party of Sokokis had been down the Saco River and was now returning to Pegwacket Village—Chief Paugus and Chief Wahwa and eighty men. They didn't know Captain Lovewell was anywhere around until they came out of the woods into this sylvan glen and found thirty-two packsacks. The Indian of that day was not highly educated and was slow at trigonometry, but he was still able to count to thirty-two, and Chief Paugus and Chief Wahwa astutely concluded there were thirty-two soldiers somewhere in the vicinity. Accordingly, they deployed their eighty-odd braves in ambush and waited.

Captain Lovewell, well documented as an astute tactician and able soldier, now led his men into the ambush like any other idiot. The stage was set for a complete massacre with one volley—but the Indians did not fire. Instead, Chief Paugus and Chief Wahwa looked at each other in astonishment, and Chief Paugus said to Chief Wahwa, "Behold! 'Tis our old friend Captain Lovewell and some of his lads. What a pleasant surprise!"

At this, the Indians came out of the bushes, and so there would be no misunderstanding they dumped the powder from the flash pans of their muskets—effectively disarming themselves in an unmistakable gesture of peace. Kindly Captain Lovewell took notice of this and, delighted with his advantage, gave an order to fire. Chief Paugus and Chief Wahwa hustled their warriors back behind trees and urged all to replenish their flash pans briskly and govern themselves accordingly. The inaccuracy of Captain Lovewell's marksmen has already been noticed, and on this occasion they did no better—they didn't get too many Indians with their first volley. Outnumbered better than two to one, Captain Lovewell's men stood there in the open glen, their guns discharged, and the first volley of the Indians wreaked fearful carnage. Captain Lovewell was killed.

After that the Indians played the waiting game, and shot only when some militiaman stuck his head up—something one does under those circumstances just once. It was a sorry affair, brought on entirely by Captain Lovewell's desire for scalps. For a time the Indians called from the woods to certain of the surviving militiamen by name, suggesting they give up. Chaplain Frye was also shot, mortally wounded, and as he lay in pain his prayers could be heard above the din that violated that sylvan serenity. Chaplains are not supposed to take part in the violence of the fray, so it was comforting to both whites and Indians that he was imploring God to take charge. God refrained, however, and after a little while Chief Paugus and Chief Wahwa withdrew, passing on to their village of Pegwacket and no doubt meditating in puzzlement over the ways of the paleface.

Thus it went with Captain Lovewell—the patriot, the Christian, the soldier, and the scalp hunter. Is it not interesting that, having won this Battle of Lovewell's Folly, the savage Indians went their way without lifting a single English scalp? Not even that of Captain Lovewell.

37

The interesting consequences of Free Will Baptism in the pious town of Hodgdon, up in Aroostook County, and how river driving became interwoven into the early pattern of religious affairs.

The Calvinistic theology of predestination struck a snag when somebody reflected that God could hardly be in favor of sin. If God sets things up and all we do is live out the lives He laid down for us, how come we mortals produce so many sinners? Many years passed before this was resolved, but one day the Hard-Shelled Baptists were lined up on one side and the Free Will Baptists on the other. Their big difference had to do with God's daily decision as to which children He would turn into saints, and which He would relegate to perdition. By

1780 New England had quite a few Free Will Baptists, although afterwards they shortened themselves to Free Baptists. In 1824 a few of these joined some New Brunswickers, and the town of Hodgdon was settled by them—until then it had been the wild land township of Groton Academy Grant.

This slightly religious twinge made Hodgdon different in the Aroostook County galaxy, where God had not always been an ever-present help in trouble, but was often outside the county on other business. So during the early days of Hodgdon the Free Baptists were an influence for good in a remote place where free will often led farmers, woodsmen, trappers, and smugglers in other directions. One of the better triumphs of frontier theology came when the Free Baptists of Hodgdon brought Charles (Rouser-Boy) Stockford to repentance and into the radiance of grace and the security of the fold.

Hodgdon is on the eastern edge of Maine, one town south of Houlton on Route One towards Calais. The place wasn't settled until 1824, when English speaking folks began working into Aroostook, but long before that the place was known to the French. In 1607 Father LeBrun had some Indians take him upriver from St. John, and he explored a number of the St. John tributaries—one of them the forty-three-mile Meduxnekeag that now runs through Hodgdon. Father LeBrun was one of the Jesuits of our early history. While in the region he climbed Mars Hill and claimed everything he could see from there for the King of France. Took in quite a territory. It might be nice to say he named Mars Hill, but he didn't. The Mars Hill on which the Apostle Paul stood to address the Athenians was not our Maine Mars

Hill. For a good many years you couldn't get to Hodgdon from here, and all going and coming was by way of New Brunswick.

The Meduxnekeag River was ample for driving lumber, and when folks did move into Hodgdon it didn't take them long to build a dam, flow a millpond, and put up a sawmill. It would be many years before enough land was logged off to give Hodgdon her big potato fields. Meantime, the Free Baptists prevailed, and they began using the millpond as a font. Not every Sunday, but as often as converts appeared, the members of the church would go to the millpond for baptismal services. It has been said that now and then a misguided convert would get his religion in the winter, and a chisel was handy for making a hole in the ice. Anybody who has ever been in Aroostook will disbelieve this very much. No Aroostookian ever got that much religion. But a pleasant summer forenoon is another matter, and when the Free Baptists held total immersion at the millpond folks came from miles and miles. Not just the Free Baptists, but spectators—sometimes a hefty housewife gave the slight but fervent minister a hard time when he retrieved her from the pond. Indeed, there had been one buoyant lady who floated off, and the reverend had to swim and tow her back. So the devotions of the Free Baptists were a good thing to see.

This Charlie Stockford was not, at the time, a Free Baptist. God had seemingly predestined him otherwise. He was tall, broad, and handsome. He was in the prime of life. He was also something of a lady's man. He was a good sport. He was reckless, carefree, dashing, and dandy. He would take a drink, and he played cards and bet on horses. He could swing an ax all day, and on the spring drives he had never fallen off his log. And on this particular baptismal Sunday, Charlie had come to the pond to watch the exercises in his best suit, new tan shoes, necktie, and a straw "boater" that was probably the first of its kind north of Newburyport. Charlie was the sort who would naturally have a new style of straw hat before anybody else. And, whereas everybody else was on the nigh side of the millpond, Charlie was conspicuous as he stood alone on the far side, at the brow of the mill where logs were brought up to the saw carriage—except that today was Sunday and the mill was down. He was a handsome sight.

The Free Baptists approached and the exercises were about to begin. The pastor waded into the pond, water to his waist. The choir arranged itself to the left. The deacons supported the young lady about to embrace the faith, and after she made her declaration of penitence they would present her to the minister for the immersion. The sun shone in magnificence, and the nonmember spectators were hushed in respectful decorum. In all the wide world of Christian piety, there was nothing that moment more sacred and hallowed than the scene at the Hodgdon millpond. The white robes of the choir proclaimed peace, and in her own baptismal robe the young lady about to receive the sacrament stood serene and hopeful, a beautiful girl radiant and pure. Across the pond, Charlie Stockford gazed, and was humble. The minister nodded, and the choir did a hymn. Then the minister said, "We are gathered . . ."

There is no knowing what possessed Charlie. He certainly had a lapse of thought. Whatever happened, he was overcome, and with his arms folded across his chest, his eyes on the young lady, he stepped from the mill brow onto a floating pine log. Without the slightest realization of what he was doing, he put his new tan Sunday shoes into motion, and in his trance he began rolling the log. Lacking spikes, his tan shoes were never meant for twirling a log, but Charlie was known as the best on the river, and he soon had the log going for fair, whipping water into the air and moving out across the pond. He still stared, and he still had his arms folded across his chest.

The baptism was forgotten. Everybody was watching Charlie. From his knees down he was in motion— above that he was a statue. The minister watched with open mouth. The young lady seemed entranced. The choir, books open, looked as one. The congregation of Free Baptists was spellbound. And all the people who had come from far and wide stood in awe. Everybody there that day had heard many times over that Charlie Stockford had never been rolled off a log. But only a few had ever seen him on a log, and here he was! Charlie at his best!

It didn't take long for Charlie's rolling log to chew its way across the small pond, and the first thing Charlie knew about the whole stunt was when something brought him out of his trance and told him it was time to reverse. He dropped his arms to his sides and looked down. He seemed bewildered, as he afterwards said he was. If he'd had his calk-soled riverman's boots, there'd have been no problem. Charlie would have dug in, the bark would have ripped, and the log would begin working the other way. But his tan Sunday shoes were no help at all. Charlie went into the drink, and there was his stylish straw hat floating away.

When Charlie splashed, the director of the choir gave the downbeat, and the Free Baptist choir sang the joyous hymn traditional at all true full-under baptisms:

Just as I am, without one plea
But that Thy blood was shed for me,
And that Thou bid'st me come to Thee,
O Lamb of God, I come.

When a town is lucky enough to have a story like
that, why does somebody bother to write a dull history
about the first grist mill, who taught first grade in 1848,
and the date of the big fire at the sawmill? Charlie
Stockford swam ashore, and the rest of his life would
twinkle his eyes upon occasion and tell how he was bap-
tized.

38

How five sincere residents of Lee had to be reprimanded for indulging after they had signed a pledge not to indulge; and a consideration of other things that have made the town of Lee outstandingly different.

Different towns acquire different fame in different ways, but the town of Lee was different. Lee is next to Lincoln, up in Penobscot County, and Lincoln was not named for Abraham—Abraham was but sixteen years old when the first people began looking at Lincoln. Nor was Lee named for Robert E., who was two years older than Abraham. Neither of those two historical gentlemen had been heard of in the upper townships at that time, but if you had inquired for Nathan, Jim, Purchase, and Stephen Lee, anybody could direct you. The Lee brothers came in 1826, having complied with the local custom of passing through Lincoln before you went to work.

This derived from an unhappy incident. The first man to come up from southern Maine to take up a lot in the "Williams College grant" found a spot that pleased him, and he went right to work clearing some fields. He was diligent and a good hand with an ax, so shortly he had the trees laid down on ten beautiful acres and was ready to put up a house and send for his family.

Then a stranger walked into his clearing, shook the man's hand, and said, "I believe you're the very first settler in the town of Lincoln."

"No," he says, "Lee."

"No, this is Lincoln."

"Can't be—I bought a lot in Lee."

"Well, this ain't Lee."

And sure enough, it ain't.

In those days nobody would want to live in Lincoln if he could live in Lee, and not too many people would today, so the poor man was distraught. It is no small thing to hew down the trees on ten acres, and now that was all behind him. True, back then there really wasn't all that much difference between this ten acres and that ten acres. All the man had to do was change his deed, and he could do that without even going to Bangor. But he was a determined and enlightened citizen and under no circumstances did he care to be a forefather of Lincoln. He picked up and packed up and went six miles farther and cleared another ten acres in Lee.

You can see that Lee has something going for it. As a grant to Williams College, Township 4, Range 2, north of Bingham's Penobscot Purchase—which is Lee—was soon dissipated in the urgent financial needs of that struggling institution. The proprietors sold out, and things began to look fine, and then one day Lee—incorporated in 1832—needed a school of its own. Accordingly, the legislature made a school grant for Lee Academy, which in turn was frittered away in academic whimsicalities. But Lee Academy did result, and as a private institution that doubles as the local high school, it stands out as unusual.

Over the years the academy has done many wonderful things for the community. One year it sent a track team downstate to compete in the state interscholastics. It had never sent a track team before; in fact Lee Academy had never had a track team. The boys just thought is might be fun, and they decided to try it. Since no school downstate had ever heard of Lee Academy, the appearance of its track team aroused some amusement. Particularly with the boys from Edward Little High School in Auburn. Edward Little took great pride in its "harriers," and for a good many years no school could even give Edward Little a contest. And this year Edward Little came as usual, expecting to breeze along, and the captain of the team already had his acceptance speech memorized for when they gave him the trophy. Well, Lee Academy beat 'em. The whole Lee team came in before the first Edward Little boy, and then the Lee team went back to Lee and began working on something else.

It may well have been the poultry show. Lee Academy is the only secondary school in the state that ever sponsored and staged a hen show. A hen show in Maine is by no means a farfetched idea. In the old days of sail, Maine sea captains brought every known breed of barnyard fowl from every port in the world, and seventy-five years ago Maine people "kept" strange and wonderful birds. A vessel due to be at sea for a couple of years would need ample provisions, and almost every deck had a chicken coop where biddies from home kept the captain, his family, and his crew reasonably well supplied with fresh eggs. When a hen quit her functional cycle, she'd go into the stew pot, and at the next port of call she would be replaced. So the Maine addiction to hens of all nations was not merely appreciation of fine feathers. Back in Maine the odd fowl took over the barnyards and it happened that almost every man who kept hens took a fancy to one breed or another so that the strains remained true.

The town of Lee never had any important poultry farming, but up and down the streets and roads you'd find Leghorns, Hamburgs, Cornish, Orpingtons, Brahmas, Minorcas, and Andalusions, as well as the Rocks and Reds and Dominiques of American origin. Too, there were geese and ducks and guinea fowl and pheasants, and about anything that could survive a voyage home. Isn't it odd that Portland, Lewiston, Bangor, with their high-riding high schools, never came up with anything so naturally Maine as a hen show? The one put on by Lee Academy was a dandy and brought crowds from all around. The second year it was much bigger and had to be moved to the Grange Hall. Meantime the smarter and higher-riding high schools around the state kept on doing the same old things.

Lee, like every other Maine town, met in annual town meeting and elected officers for the coming year. Today a town will elect its selectmen, a clerk, treasurer, collector, road commissioner, and then leave what are known as "minor" town officers to be appointed by the selectmen. In the beginning this was not so, and everybody voted for all officers, major and minor. The minor officers include fence viewers, field driver, pound keeper, hog reeve, sealers and scalers of various commodities, and coastal towns always name a harbor master. Harbor masters still are needed, but most of the duties of minor officers have become obsolete and they don't get appointed now. Or, if a need arises, the selectmen serve. It's been years since any Maine town had a serious, old-time, line fence dispute, where adjacent landowners can't agree as to which shall build what. If such a dispute arose, the selectmen would no doubt name themselves fence viewers and proceed.

Well, as the need for these minor officers declined, and towns stopped electing and appointing them, the town of Lee with characteristic and laudable difference looked at the situation in its own way. The hog reeve is an officer whose duty is to round up stray hogs and turn them over to the pound keeper. The pound keeper, in turn, feeds the animals until an owner claims them, and then exacts a fee for the animals' care and a punitive fine. There had been no civic necessity in the town of Lee for such services in a great many years, but what difference does that make? The inhabitants of Lee qualified to vote in town affairs began electing the town's most recent bridegroom as hog reeve. They kept this up for a good many years, and then shifted to fence viewer.

So Lee, you see, merits attention and respect for reasons not usually put forth. Its fame does not depend entirely on being next to Lincoln. In 1879 the enthusiasm of the good people of Lee for the prohibition policies of Neal Dow caused them to organize a strong lodge of the Independent Order of Good Templars. With a population of less than 900, Lee turned out 119 fervent "white ribboners"—each and every Good Templar pledged to abstain entirely from intoxicating beverages.

It cost a man fifty cents to join; a woman, twenty-five cents. Quarterly dues were fifteen cents. Fervor ran high, and Demon Rum was on the skids. But by the time of the May meeting, in 1880, the shine seemed to be wearing off. At that meeting the members took a deep breath and kicked out five Good Templars who had been caught drinking cider.

39

A most amusing, but short, anecdote about Moses and Isaac Hodsdon and how they successfully reconciled their difference of opinion, going on to make their marks gracefully in state affairs.

Twelve miles out of Bangor is the town of Kenduskeag, but you could miss it. Small as it is, it nurtured two sons worth our attention. First, Moses Hodsdon, who went up there as a young man to survey what was then Lot 1, Range 8. He liked the place, bought some land, and moved on. He was thus the first settler and became its first citizen, a good friend to and a big help for others who came later. He became Kenduskeag's first postmaster, and this was a good thing because he could read. Nobody else in town could read, so when Moses handed you a letter he could tell you what it said. Fact is that

Moses was one of these people who can do just about anything—he'd mastered all the crafts, and we've seen that he was a surveyor. Some say Kenduskeag comes from the Indian and means a place to catch eels. This has never been seriously disputed.

Moses Hodsdon was the oldest child in a family of twelve, and after a few years he brought his younger brother Isaac to live with him at Kenduskeag. Isaac was number nine in that family, and he and Moses were to become the two sons of Kenduskeag worth our attention. Moses put Isaac into the local school, which had just lately been started, and immediately it was discovered that Isaac had an embarrassing physical infirmity. He was left-handed! It was a great disgrace for any family to have a lefty, and the teacher went right to work in a gallant effort to shift Isaac over and make him normal. But Isaac was a stubborn little rascal, and he wouldn't give in. After the school year the teacher had to turn Isaac loose as an unreformed pupil, and his brother Moses took over in an effort to bring Isaac from sinister to dexter and preserve the reputation of the family. All summer Moses had at it, but Isaac was still stubborn.

Moses went into his shop and made a ferule of black walnut. Possibly, today, the ferule should be explained. It was a wooden stick used to gain the attention of reluctant students, and it hurt like the very devil. Little girls, sugar and spice, never needed the ferule, but every little boy would sooner or later be invited to go belly flops on his desk, and Teacher would make him smart. Sometimes Teacher would make a boy hold out his hand, palm up, and she'd whack him a good one. A ferule would, if applied to the knuckles, crack them. So Moses began whacking Isaac with the ferule every time he caught his little brother doing anything with his left hand, and after a little of that Isaac took the ferule and burned it in the stove.

Then Moses went and cut a "soople" switch. The word is supple, but every Maine boy was brought up on soople—he'd be invited to go and cut a soople switch, and then his mother would just about cut his legs off at the knees as she taught him right from wrong and led him into the paths of righteousness. Moses did get a few whacks in, but Isaac took the soople switch down and threw it into the Penobscot River. He continued to use his left hand.

It is good to know the two brothers came to a workable compromise. Isaac agreed to learn to write with his right hand if he might be permitted to dip the pen into the inkwell with his left.

In 1819 Moses Hodsdon was sent down from Kenduskeag as a delegate to the constitutional convention—Maine was about to be separated from Massachusetts and needed a constitution. It was a proud day when the folks of wee Kenduskeag gave him three cheers as he set out. So the signature of Moses Hodsdon is in the archives and may be admired for its firm lines.

In 1841 Isaac Hodsdon also came downstate, and was Adjutant General of Maine—another great honor for Kenduskeag. So his forceful signature, right-handed, is also on record and may be seen. People from other departments in the statehouse used to peek into Isaac's office when he was signing papers. They were amused to see him write, and then shift the pen to his left hand and dip it.

40

A chronicle of some of the enterprises of the Stanley twins of Kingfield, and a small digression that tells of the important part Maine played in the development of the X-ray, and Perley Watson's rash.

It's pretty hard to get in and out of Kingfield before somebody there tells you again about the wonderful Stanley twins and their gifted sister, but as usual with all good stories relegated to historical inertia, most of the human side of the Stanleys has been pared away in favor of facts, statistics, and dry rot. The Stanley twins were, all the same, comical cusses who got a lot of fun out of life, and since they were capable of just about everything else, it stands to reason they could have worked out a juggling act and gone on the vaudeville circuit. They didn't. The facts are plentiful, and they begin in Kingfield.

Their father, Squire Stanley, came to Kingfield as a friend of William King, Maine's first governor and one of the proprietors of Township 3R1 BKP WKR, which was to become Kingfield, named for the governor. Governor King helped develop the township and lived there for a time, and besides the Stanleys he brought numerous other friends to the Carrabasset Valley. Mother and Father Stanley had seven children, but four of the boys customarily get ignored. The twins, Francis E. and Freelan O., were born in Kingfield on June 1, 1849. The only sister, Chansonetta, would become famous in her own right as a photographer, and her reputation as a good one depends not at all on her genius brothers.

Complete look-alikes, Francis and Freelan grew up in Kingfield and showed promise from the beginning. They were still boys when they turned simple whittling to good use and turned out violins. Stanley violins were used by the Boston Symphony Orchestra! After that they tried all manner of things, and all turned out the finest kind. When gas came along, for fuel and illumination, the twins developed a home gas generator. It worked all right, but community gas companies came into being and the householder didn't need to make his own. The boys turned elsewhere with their talents. Kingfield always took great interest in what the twins were doing, and now word ran around that they were perfecting a new kind of photographic plate. Before that all such plates were "wet," and a photographer had to flow one before he could make a picture and develop it immediately after exposure. It took a horse and wagon to carry a photographer's camera and darkroom equipment about, and it also took a lot of time to produce a picture.

The sister, Chansonetta, was able to give her brothers technical advice. When the Stanley Dryplate was perfected, in 1883, twin Francis went down to Lewiston and set up a factory to mass produce it. This was in 1883, and soon twin Freelan came down to join his brother. Success was immediate, and then the twins moved to Newton, Massachusetts, where they would remain. It wasn't long before the growing Eastman Kodak company yearned for the Stanley Dryplate and sent a man around to sound the twins out. The twins knew very well what they had, and they were jealous of its quality.

They set a figure that suited them, and Kodak never regretted meeting it, but they stipulated that their emulsion be put only on glass until such time as a comparable "film" could be produced. The twins, and Eastman, knew full well that "film" would some day replace breakable glass, but at that time no celluloid, isinglass, and any form of what we call plastics had sufficient clarity to suit the delicate Stanley emulsion. It was to be many years before chemists could meet the Stanley restriction, and meantime Eastman Kodak scrupulously used the finest glass obtainable. Sister Chansonetta, using Stanley plates to obtain her incomparable effects, was proof enough this restriction was a wise one. Having sold their dryplate patents to Kodak, the Stanley twins turned to find something else to play with. They took up X-ray.

Roentgen rays were discovered in 1895, but it would be some years before they became more than a physicist's plaything. Tubes to create the rays had to be perfected, and in this matter Maine took a part on this side of the Atlantic Ocean. Dr. Gilbert M. Elliott, a general practitioner in Brunswick, was a subscriber to a German scientific journal. Since Dr. Elliott couldn't read German, it served no purpose (he admitted one time) beyond impressing patients in his waiting room. But looking through it he found an article about X-rays, and he carried the magazine over to Professor Charles Hutchins, who headed the physics department at Bowdoin College. Dr. Hutchins was not a medical man, but he could read German. A few days later Drs. Hutchins and Elliott met on the street, and Dr. Hutchins said, "I've made one of those tubes from the magazine, maybe you'd like to come up to the lab and see it work?"

When X-rays were first announced as a news item, laws were proposed to ban them. A woman wouldn't be safe walking along the sidewalk if somebody could turn on a lamp and look right through her clothes! That didn't bother Drs. Hutchins and Elliott, and for a long time after that Dr. Hutchins had a monopoly in making X-ray tubes—he sold them to all the labs in the country, making them in the instrument shop on Bowdoin campus. The first photograph Dr. Hutchins made during his experimentations was of Dr. Elliott's hand—showing his bones and his Masonic ring. It is extant.

Then one day a certain Perley Watson, respected resident of Brunswick, came into Dr. Elliott's office to complain about an ache in his back. Perley worked for the railroad, and he thought he might have lifted something that threw his back "out of kilter." Dr. Elliott felt Perley all over, consoled him, stuck on a support, and prescribed care. "Come in again if it doesn't get better," he said.

Perley did come in again, and insisted he was worse

off than Dr. Elliott knew. And since X-rays were the talk of the day, he said, "Why don't you take my picture with that X-ray machine and find out what's askew?" When Dr. Elliott asked Dr. Hutchins what he thought about a picture of Perley's back, the answer was that it would need a big photographic plate, and so far nobody knew how long an exposure would have to be. "Why'n't we try it?" said Dr. Hutchins.

Perley was willing, so they put a pillow under his head and arranged him over a huge wet plate, protected from other light. Dr. Hutchins turned on the X-ray tube and waited the supposed exposure time. All went well. Perley's belly came out fine, and Dr. Elliott could see nothing wrong with Perley's backbone. He told Perley to continue to take things easy. Thus assured, Perley was pleased, and offered to pay Dr. Hutchins for taking his picture. "No, this is just experimental, and I'm not in the business—unless you want to donate a few pennies to cover the cost of the plate." Perley gave Dr. Hutchins five dollars.

That was the first use of X-ray by a physician, anywhere—the value of X-ray in surgery wasn't recognized in Europe for quite some time. A week later Perley Watson was back in Dr. Elliott's office with a new problem. "Doc," he said, "I got a rash on my belly and it itches like hell." Dr. Elliott gave him a skin lotion, but the next time he and Dr. Hutchins met, Dr. Hutchins held out his hand and said, "Look! Those X-rays burn. We've got to be careful." Dr. Elliott never told Perley Watson about X-ray burns, and was greatly relieved after some weeks when Perley's stomach rash subsided by itself.

This digression is meant to show the state of affairs with X-rays at the time the Stanley twins took an inter-

est in them. A whole era of X-ray technology was about
to open, and with their talents the twins might have led
the procession. They knew about the experiments of
Dr. Hutchins and owned one of his tubes. But just previously they had seen a De Dion Bouton newly imported
from France, and they became enchanted with the idea
of making motor cars. They lost interest in X-rays.

The Stanley Steamer thus came into production. It
would be the first mass-produced automobile; until that
time every automobile was a thing by itself. Henry Ford
would add the "assembly line" later, but in the Stanley
factory every man had his own part to handle and every
part he made was like every other he made. When a
Stanley Steamer climbed the dirt road to the top of
Mount Washington in New Hampshire in just about
two hours, the publicity put the Stanley Steamer plant
in high gear. The twins had made their two-hundredth
car when they began receiving solid offers for their patents. Not caring to sell, they tried to discourage buyers
by setting a high price—a quarter of a million dollars!
Undaunted, a man came with papers to sign and the
money, and using the Stanley patents the Locomobile
Corporation was founded and began making steamers.

Now the brothers looked about again to find something to do, and one Stanley twin said to the other Stanley twin, "A better automobile can be made." So they
made one. Ignoring the patents they had just sold, they
brought forth a new kind of machine. The chain drive
was gone, there was a new lubrication system, the boiler
was different. It was an entirely new vehicle, without
infringing in any way on the patents they had sold to
Locomobile, but it made the Locomobile steamer obsolete. Locomobile quit, and a happy arrangement was
made whereby the Stanley twins bought back the use-

less patents in a gesture of good will. They were good boys.

When the Stanley twins were at their peak, some union out in Indiana sent an organizer to bring the workers into the fold, and there was the usual demand for better working conditions and twenty-five cents more. The Stanley twins had their own ideas about everything, and they met this head-on. Well, they never made any guarantee on anything—if it had their name on it you could depend on them; a good product doesn't need guarantees. There was no credit in their business, either—you paid cash before you drove away. And the twins worked in the factory along with their people, they knew what every man was good for. So they told their people to forget about a union, and to come in one at a time and talk things over. "If you're worth another quarter, we'll pay it," they said. As long as they were in business, the Stanley operation was never unionized. It was the internal combustion engine that brought an end to the Stanley Steamer.

All of which the good folks in Kingfield like to recite, and they give you a solid history of two solid boys who came down off the hill and made a big success. Somehow the stories of the Stanley twins never convey that they were just country boys at heart and loved their fun. Well, after they were long established in Newton, well-to-do, well known, and secure in respectable estimation, they loved to take a little time off and ride about Greater Boston to bait policemen. The twins looked alike, and both sported the same cut of whisker.

One of them would start out in a Stanley Steamer and go hunting for an innocent policeman walking his beat and minding his own business. Understand, the Stanley Steamer didn't tear down the road with the exhaust pipe roaring, but could attain good mph with just the swish-swish of its steam propulsion. The only noise it made was with the squeeze bulb of the horn. Having found a victim, the twin would rev up and come along ahead of a great cloud of dust, squeezing his horn and contriving to make the policeman stop him as a public menace. Motor vehicle traffic was in its infancy, and sometimes a car didn't go by in a week. The policeman relished the encounter and would give his little lecture on prudence and caution. Just then the other twin would go kiting past, and the first twin would ask the cop if maybe he wasn't confused about his identifications. It wasn't easy to tell which twin was which when they were driving identical cars. Then they'd go looking for another cop.

Appropriate or not, twin Francis died in an automobile accident on the Newburyport Turnpike on July 31, 1918. Twin Freelan lived on without incident into his nineties—he died October 2, 1940. The twins will not soon be forgotten in their native Kingfield—nor at the antique car rallies, where a Stanley Steamer always steals the show.

41

The most interesting chronicle of the centennial observance of the righteous town of Litchfield, which staged a mammoth celebration that refrained entirely from wantonness and iniquity.

Even in our most hilarious and frenetic moments of gladness, Maine people have ever been guardians of the proper, and restraint against iniquity, evil, sin, and open cavorting has been our righteous anchor to windward. A fine example is the way the town of Litchfield went about its centennial observance. Litchfield is in the mid-country between Gardiner and Lewiston, and folks who rode the Androscoggin & Kennebec Electric Railway often went right through Litchfield and didn't know it. The community has three somewhat villages—Litchfield, Litchfield Corners, and Litchfield Plains. Litchfield has always been one of those hometowns that produce excellent citizens for the world away, and there is no corner of a foreign field that can't turn you up a true Litchfieldite if you look around. Litchfield Fair continues to be one of Maine's best; old friends meet there in early September. Litchfield is not the community on whose pulse the State of Maine depends, but those who love it are loyal and numerous. The population today hefts a thousand, and the town's lakes add some summercaters.

Litchfield was settled as Smithfield and later called Smithtown, but was incorporated as Litchfield on February 18, 1795, as the ninety-third Maine town.

So when 1895 approached, the good people of Litchfield considered having a bang-up centennial observance, and they did. At the March town meeting in 1894 the warrant included article 3—concerning a celebration. Article 1 was to elect a moderator, and article 2 was to receive and approve the town reports, so article 3 was really the first order of business. A wing-ding was accordingly approved, and it was held on August 21, 1895. It was one of the finest programs ever staged by any Maine community, and when darkness settled over Litchfield everybody was exhausted. In 1895 the Litchfield Fair was already thirty-five years old, so the fairgrounds made an ideal place to stage the ceremonies. Against the possibility of inclement weather, the huge tent of the Kennebec Camp Meeting Association was rented and raised, with a capacity of three-thousand people. Bands came, there was choral singing, they had cannon, and nothing was spared. Everybody in town was in the parade.

The committee took the liberty of inviting anybody and everybody who might lend something to the occasion, so the list of invited guests was impressive and quite a few of them came. Governor Cleaves came, but had to leave early. Indeed, so many dignitaries came that time ran out and some of them didn't get to speak—Congressman Nelson Dingley and former governor Frederick Robie, to name two. All former governors had been invited, governors of other states, representatives from all other towns, sundry college presidents and divines, and even a Kentucky colonel! Distinguished dozens sent regrets and best wishes, and one might say the Litchfield Centennial was outstanding for the important people who didn't come. It took better than an hour to read all the regrets.

There was one untoward incident. The weather of the day was bright, but windy. Midway of the program one side of the big tent blew away. Nobody was hurt, but the flapping of the canvas was an unscheduled interruption. After this distraction the exercises moved to the fair's bandstand, and after more regrets the quartet sang again. Everything was a great success and shows, in a way, that you can have fun without smoking and drinking.

Well—to return to the town meeting of March 1894, and the action under article 3: "To see what action the town will take for the proper observance of the 100th anniversary of the incorporation of the town, February 18, 1895, and act anything thereto."

That's pretty broad authorization, and the town voted aye on five motions:

1. Voted to celebrate.
2. Voted to choose a committee of seven to arrange for said celebration.
3. Voted that the selectmen (3), the superintending school committee (3), and the town treasurer (1) serve as said committee, they to add further members if needed.

4. Voted to raise and appropriate $100 to cover expenses of said celebration.
5. On motion of the Reverend James Richmond, revered pastor of the Litchfield church, it was voted that in their arrangements for said celebration the committee shall not include any dancing.

Thus the iniquity of Litchfield was kept within due bounds, and the program was entirely serene and righteous—so much so that the pious members of the Ladies' Grange Society approved and immediately added $25 to the celebration fund. Later, at a special town meeting, another $200 was appropriated by the citizens, making a total centennial celebration fund with the frugal figure of $325—but there was no dancing.

42

The death of Captain Moor of HMS *Margaretta* is recounted, with some other information about the Battle of Machias, and the details of how the captain precipitously departed divine worship.

Here's one to think about! Ask any patriotic American about the Battle of Concord and Lexington, or about the Battle of Bunker Hill, and you'll get the full recitation. But ask any patriotic American about the Battle of Machias, and he'll likely say, "Where's Machias?" Machias is right where it always was, and that's away Down East in Maine. It's the shire town of the sunrise county of Washington, and that means in colonial days it was closer to Halifax than to Boston—Halifax being the base of British operations during our American Revolution. And while the good folks of Machias kept a somewhat chummy relationship with Halifax, they were no less true patriots, and they did their part—although one historian lamented that the facts are scarcely known outside the locality itself. What story out of Concord and Lexington, or out of Bunker Hill, can top the escape of the British admiral when he jumped out the church window between the offertory and the epistle?

"Machias" comes from the Indian word for the falls on the river now called Machias, as near as English can come to what a Frenchman heard when an Indian said *Mechises*. The word is pronounced something like Muh-chigh-'s. Years ago, in the halcyon days of radio, most people far Down East listened to station WBZ in Boston. WBZ had a clear channel with fifty-thousand watts power, and the signal zipped over the water of the Gulf of Maine to boom into homes better than those of stations closer by. The news editor of WBZ knew that he had this down-Maine audience, so he would try to find items about that area to work into his newscasts. It was accordingly fun to tune in WBZ and hear the announcer say, "Mack-ee-ass, Maine—Selectmen here have announced, etc., etc." There were several people on the staff of WBZ who well knew how to pronounce Machias in the down-Maine way, but they pleasantly refrained from correcting the news staff, and WBZ continued for some time to say mack-ee-ass while Down-Easters smiled.

Unlike most early Maine settlements, fish, farming, and furs had little to do with the beginnings of Machias. The Machias River with its water power and its long valley of standing timber brought exploiters, and they put up a sawmill long before they had a church. Even up to the American Revolution, Machias still wasn't growing its own food, and vessels brought even potatoes from Halifax. But the whine of the sawmill was music, and Machias had a prosperity while other settlements struggled.

In 1904 George Drisko, the historian of Machias, wrote that he found no satisfactory record or evidence of discovery or settlement in the Machias area before 1605. Not too many Maine places bother to look that far back, but Historian Drisko was wrong. In 1527 John Rutt, master of the schooner *Mary of Guilford*, liked the looks of that region, wrote about it, and drew a map, or chart, that shows him an able cartographer. He also "erected a cross," which makes Machias a member of the club. Not knowing (it seems) about the Rutt visit, Drisko says there was a trading post on Clark's Point in 1606—the year before the "firsts" of Jamestown and Popham. Machias is in that "Acadia" disputed for so many years by England and France, so the actual settlement of the place by any English didn't come about until 1763.

When Machias did start, it went off with a bang. The second year of its being, 1764, the sawmills of Machias turned out 1,600,000 board feet of lumber. In short, Machias quickly became a major American town. The first drive of sawlogs on the Machias River began an annual series that ended two centuries later with the last—the first and last in America. Looking ahead, the fomenters of the American Revolution stationed three-hundred militiamen at Machias, as a frontier guard against British approaches from Halifax.

The Machias "Liberty Pole" has words between the lines. Why would anybody in Machias know anything about the colonial custom of raising a Liberty Pole to protest the tyranny of George III? Away down there? Not at all—vessels traded at Machias, bringing food and supplies to a prosperous community, and Machias lumber was sent wherever people would buy it. Away down there, Machias was aware of what was going on, and two days after the Battle of Concord and Lexington the folks at Machias knew all about it. And they didn't like it. So they put up a Liberty Pole. In some sophisticated places around Boston, and perhaps in Connecticut, it took a little doing to get a Liberty Pole in place, but to the lumbermen of Machias it took but a few minutes. A crew went into the woods and fetched a pine of the right size, and while they were gone another crew dug a hole. The pine was limbed out so a tuft remained at the top, and up she went—"Gaffle on, there, and now all h'ist!" Thus Machias affirmed its love for freedom and liberty, and their Liberty Pole touched off the first naval battle of our Revolutionary War. Pity you never heard about that.

The Battle of Concord and Lexington came on April 19. Along about the last of April three vessels from Halifax arrived in the river at Machias and dropped anchor. Two were schooners, and the third was a naval escort cutter under the command of a Captain Moor. Captain Moor was under orders to get the two schooners loaded with Machias lumber, and to have the cargo delivered to Boston where it would be used to build housing for British soldiers. Since there was a long-standing, and heretofore friendly, rapport between Machias and Halifax, war or not, Captain Moor was pleasantly received, and he was affable. He stated his errand, the lumbermen of Machias told him there was no way. King George didn't have money enough for that kind of lumber. Sorry, but not really. At this, Captain Moor pointed at the Liberty Pole, making it his symbolic excuse; and he told them this was open rebellion, and they'd have to take it down. He said if it didn't come down, he'd have to

unlimber his guns and blast Machias into smithereens.
Take it or leave it, boards or no boards, this was it!

"Well," they said, "we thank you for your frank words,
and we'll have to hold a meeting and decide what to do.
Meantime, enjoy your stay."

The lumber dealers of Machias then withdrew and
talked things over, but instead of making arrangements
to take down the pole they discussed the defense of
Machias and what they should do to be saved. When
Captain Moor demanded to know their decision, they
said, "We got to hold a town meeting—this isn't something just us few should decide." So that took a few
days, and in the meantime messengers went to settlements nearby and to the islands, asking everybody to
come and bring his musket, and also word went to the
Passamaquoddy Indians—who turned out to be a big
help. The town meeting, when it was finally held, voted
to keep the pole where it was, and fie on George III.
Then came Sunday, and word ran about that Captain
Moor would attend church.

The Machias people recognized an opportunity, and
they decided to take Captain Moor prisoner and thus
resolve things, and plans were laid accordingly. The
church was a new one, and instead of pews it had simple benches made of good Machias planks, and they were
arranged Anglican fashion so there was a wide aisle down
the middle. John O'Brien agreed to muckle the captain,
and would be sitting so he could do this. Others would
dispose themselves so they could help, and things should
come off swimmingly.

And it came to pass, and Captain Moor rowed ashore
from the anchored *Margaretta*, his cutter, and left his
skiff at the town wharf, and arrived at church to take
his place. We don't know if the minister had been tipped

off or not, but he took the pulpit at the appointed time and commenced the devotions. As things progressed, and John O'Brien was awaiting the signal to jump on Captain Moor, the captain chanced to look out the church window, which was open because of the congenial spring weather, and saw his *Margaretta* securely at anchor with lookouts alert. Beyond her, downriver, the sun sparkled on blue Maine water, and the scene was serene and lovely. Then he saw a lot of men coming up the shore, headed into town, and each was bringing his musket. The men from settlements nearby, and from the islands, and the Passamaquoddy Indians were arriving. Captain Moor saw this, and just as John O'Brien was about to spring, Captain Moor rose from his plank and dove through the open window, leaving the minister in mid-sentence. And, also, leaving the conspirators foiled. John O'Brien shrugged his shoulders and made a gesture of frustration. Captain Moor picked himself up and raced for the wharf, gaining his skiff and rowing for the *Margaretta*. True, he wasn't really an admiral, but he was a British officer in command, and that's better than Concord and Bunker Hill can claim.

Before things were resolved the Machias boys captured the *Margaretta*, and in the skirmish the only British naval officer ever to jump through a Machias church window was killed. There were other casualties on both sides, and it's interesting that a boat was sent to Halifax to fetch a surgeon to attend the wounded. The Machias folks might be mad at England, but Halifax was still Halifax. A surgeon did come, Dr. William Chaloner, and he did what he could for the wounded. Then, he liked the place, and he decided to stay in Machias, where he practiced to the end of his days.

The taking of the *Margaretta* became the first naval

engagement of the Revolutionary War. It took place five days before the Battle of Bunker Hill. At Halifax the British authorities said this was the work of "a piratical band," which may have fooled the king but wasn't taken seriously in Machias. In "retaliation" a fleet was sent to reduce Machias and teach everybody a good lesson, and no doubt to get some boards, and then they had a real battle, which the English lost. There were a couple of incidents in this battle that Concord and Lexington might relish.

The fight was between ships afloat and soldiers on land. At one moment a group of Machias folks came boldly out of the woods near one of the warships, and it seemed innocent enough. It seemed to be a company of mourners with a casket on a small cart, the casket covered with a piece of sailcloth, and the group wheeled the cart down to a level spot. The English supposed it was a funeral, and paid no further heed. But when the exercises began, the mourners whipped the sailcloth away, and the casket turned out to be a twelve-pounder, with which the mourners blew the transom off the warship.

The Battle of Machias also established the marksmanship of Chief Francis Joseph Neptune of the Quoddies. Chief Neptune already had a reputation as a sharpshooter, and now he pointed at an English officer on the poop of a warship, and he said without modesty, "I could pick him off from right here!" The distance was too great; he was told he couldn't do it and to forget about it. Chief Neptune insisted. "Let me try," he said. "I'll show you."

"Aw, go on . . . ," they said.

"Let me try—hand me a gun!"

So they gave him a musket, and Chief Neptune aimed

most carefully before he pulled the trigger. The ball went high, over the officer's head.

Chief Neptune brushed aside the comical remarks addressed to him and said, "I computed the trajectory without proper kinetic adjustment. I'll get him next time."

"Aw, go on. . . ."

"Let me have another gun!"

This time the chief got his trajectory in hand, and the English officer fell overboard with a ball through his heart. Unfortunate that one historian dismisses all this with the simple note that "several friendly Indians took part in this engagement." So they did, and when the real fight began, brought on when Chief Neptune nailed the officer, the howls and whoops of the Quoddies greatly confused the English soldiers—they'd skulk along the shore, hiding behind trees, and the soldiers on the ships thought there were yelps enough for at least a million.

The "retaliation" was a failure, and back at Halifax after a strategic retreat Sir George Collier, British commandant at Halifax, put it on record that "the damned rebels at Machias were a harder set than those at Bunker Hill." And the Provincial Congress, sitting at Cambridge, sent a vessel on a special trip, to deliver to the people of Machias the "resolution" it had just passed—a citation commending the citizens of Machias on their complete success in the first naval battle of the War of Independence. The Liberty Pole was still in place. And not one stick of Machias lumber was ever used to house a Redcoat at Boston.